Keys to Cash Flow

A Covered Call Strategy

Leroy W. Hartman, Jr.

creative
rights

An imprint of
Artist Eye Books

Printed and bound in the United States of America.

Keys to Cash Flow: A Covered Call Strategy
ISBN 978-1-937966-04-1

www.financialleadershiptraining.com

Published by Creative Rights Publishing, an imprint of Artist Eye Books.
artisteyebooks@gmail.com

Cover spine by Heather Lowry, heatherlowrydesign.com.
Front cover photo courtesy of dreamstime.com, used with permission.

Dedicated to my wife, Traci, whose unwavering support has enabled my personal trading interests to become a reality.

Disclaimer: Trading involves risk, including the possible loss of principle and other losses. Your trading results may vary. No representations are being made that these techniques will result in or guarantee profits in trading. Past performance is no indication of future results.

Foreword:

Learning from the Experience of Others is the Short-Cut to Success

by D. Scott Elder, co-founder of Investools, Inc.

I have known Leroy Hartman for more than ten years. We first became acquainted when he came to work at Investools, the investing education company I co-founded, as an instructor. After selling Investools I was the co-founder of another company that developed and fulfilled investing education programs for brokerage firms. Leroy was asked to join us and be a partner in that company and to be in charge of the development of the stock and options trading programs for our clients.

Leroy has a passion for teaching people how to improve their financial circumstances. What is remarkable about him is that, unlike many in this field of educating people how to be successful traders, he sincerely cares about people and feels a stewardship in helping people achieve success. Leroy has invested countless hours of his life refining his trading skills to distil down from his research and experience what actually works --and why.

But being a skilled trader is not enough. If you want to teach other people how to be successful traders, you have to also be a skilled teacher. This is where others in the investor education field fall short, way short. And this is where Leroy stands above others. He has also invested a good deal of his life in refining his teaching skills. Leroy can transfer his many years of research and experience to his students in concise, clear and easy to understand approach that enables anyone to more quickly and easily achieve success. He can take his personal learning curve of many years and compress it down into just a few hours for his students. That's what you get when you purchase this book, Leroy's years of experience compressed down for you to immediately profit from it, not to mention the price on this book is a small fraction of its true value.

We quickly learned at Investools that covered call cash flow strategies were the favorite trading strategy of our students, and for a very good reason. Knowing how to find and invest in good solid stocks is the foundation of investing in stocks. Learning how to do covered calls on these stocks is like turning the stock into a rental property - every month, money can literally flow into your account. And as someone who has owned rental property, I can attest that covered calls are a much better way to go. You don't have to maintain them, repair them, deal with collecting delinquent rents and all of the other headaches that come with owning rental property. You buy the stock, you write the call, and the money automatically flows in. And since it's not considered a high-risk investing strategy you're allowed to do it in your self-directed IRA accounts.

The key is knowing how to find the best stocks for doing covered calls, what call contract to trade on the stock, and then how to manage your trades in order to maximize your profit. This is what Leroy shows you how to do, step-by-by step. This book is so amazingly thorough. Leroy spares no effort to dig down deep into the mechanics of covered call investing. When you finish this book, you will know how to successfully generate consistent and reliable cash flow through covered calls. And by so doing, you will feel a deep sense of gratitude to Leroy for enriching your life through sharing with you in this book what has taken him years to refine.

Introduction:

Looking at the markets as a way to secure the retirement you have worked so hard to build is one of the sub-headings next to apple pie in *The American Way*. Before handing over your nest egg to the young broker on Wall Street in hopes of landing on Easy Street, consider how you arrived at this point in the first place.

Your lifelong hard work has put you in a position to make another monumental decision that will affect the rest of your life. When you started your career, you did not have all the answers, but with the correct training and knowledge you were able to buy a home, raise a family and even throw in a vacation or two over the years. Now, armed with the right amount of knowledge, you can properly invest your money. The truth is no one cares about your money or retirement quite like you. Mainly because you understand what risk you are willing to assume to remain or become retired.

Before you run to the nearest book store and buy every stock market investing book, decide what you really want out of investing. Did you know that investing and trading are two different approaches to the market? Are you familiar with risk in the market place as it refers to buying stock, options or other investing vehicles?

Having traveled the world for the past decade teaching individuals how to make money trading online, I'm constantly amazed by the fact that virtually every person I meet wants to own a business to generate consistent monthly cash flow so they can improve their lifestyle or standard of living. In my opinion, this is the universal desire of nearly every ambitious person in the world. We all want to be living the lifestyle of our dreams and be in control of our own destiny, but few understand how to do it, or even where to start.

The following strategy may be the easiest and most powerful way for you to accomplish your goal of generating a consistent monthly income from a business you own. I've been using these strategies for years and I know they work if you will be patient and stick to this simple plan.

It may not surprise you but the business I'm talking about is trading in the stock market. Most people think the stock market is just a place for the rich to get richer and the poor to get poorer. I honestly feel that trading in the stock market is one of the very few ways an average person can reach some level of financial security in their lifetime without having to start out with lots of money. Granted, you will not be living in luxury off the profits of trading if you start out with a small account balance, but you can begin to accumulate profits so it can become a reality sooner than later.

If you treat trading like a hobby, as most investors do, it will only pay you like a hobby. I don't know about you, but most of my hobbies end up *costing* me money, not *making* me money. The reason I make this comparison is that I've always been impressed with the passion people have for their individual hobbies. It takes that kind of passion for your trading to turn it into a business.

I don't want to give you the expectation that everyone makes money in the stock market because it simply isn't true. What I can say is that most traders who make impressive amounts of money on a consistent basis are passionate about trading. They have a plan and they stick to it. They are not swayed by everything they see on TV or read in the newspaper or some financial newsletter. They have tremendous focus and discipline. If something works well for them, they become a master at it rather than trying to jump to the next fad.

The other challenge of turning investing into a business is that it takes time and requires patience. There is no shortcut to wealth that doesn't involve tremendous risk. There will be ups and downs along the way that must be endured and losses that must be recovered.

However, there's simply no better business to be in than the business of trading. I can do everything I need to do to run my trading business right from my home or from any computer that can get me connected to the Internet. I've no employees to worry about and no boss giving me orders. I work when I want and it's far from hard labor. I rarely spend an average of more than an hour a day and consistently earn an executive level income each year from my trading and investments.

As a trader and/or investor you are basically in the business of selling. I know many people hate the thought of selling something. The mere mention of the word conjures up images of vacuum salesmen knocking on our door or telesales calling us at dinnertime to re-mortgage our home or sell us insurance. In the business of trading we're going to look at selling from an entirely different perspective.

Probably the best thing about my trading business is that nobody can set a limit on how much money I can make. This is one business that truly has *unlimited potential*. If you don't make all the money you want in your business, you can take it up with the guy you see in the mirror each morning. I'll also bet you didn't realize that some of the highest paid people in the world are salesman. Having run a number of successful marketing companies, I can attest to the fact that the salesman are almost always the highest paid in the company, often earning more than the owners or senior executives with amounts easily in the 6 figure range.

The biggest difference between you and the average sales person, though, is that you never have to worry about finding a buyer for what you want to sell. The stock market is designed to offer a fair and liquid place to trade stocks, so there's always a buyer at a fair price waiting for someone willing to sell.

So what's the secret to generating cash flow from your portfolio? Let me show you.

Chapter 1

One, Two, Three…Can it be that Easy?

Compared to investing, which will be referred to throughout this book as a stock that is held for 1 year or longer, trading of stocks alone can be much more demanding of your time-something you may feel you don't have enough of. Even though it demands more time, many trade stocks and options on a shorter term basis (less than 1 year) because of the opportunity for obtaining profits more quickly as well as the potential for larger profits. The goal of the 3-Step Process is to reduce the amount of time spent generating cash flow for consistent account growth, regardless of market conditions.

The 3-Step Process is built through years of experience, the refinement of trading strategies and technical chart reading skills.

3-Step Trading Process

1) Search
2) Research
3) Manage

Step 1: Search

Searching for stocks or options to invest in successfully has often troubled many Traders. Someone just starting to execute their first stock investment may look to those they trust to have the *hot stocks*. This can mean opening a financial newspaper, tuning into the business radio station to and from work each day, turning on the streaming quote cable T.V. channel, walking into the nearest big name brokerage firm or simply asking your neighbor, who happens to talk about stocks all the time. The fact is each of these is a viable source to find *possible* stocks to trade.

Before the *hot stock* or security to trade suggestion can be traded, it must fit into your personal risk threshold and trading strategies. Many of the *hot stocks* come from a recommendation that follows a successful trade or investment. What is successful? In trading, it is when a trade goes as planned and money was profited because of the transaction. Advice from all the sources named earlier is generally given on the heels of success. Regardless of the source, if the shoe fits, or in our case if the security meets the requirements searched for, then trade it!

Step 2: Research

Research is a detail orientated deciphering of pages and pages of financial data reflecting a publicly traded company to determine the optimum entry or exit based on chart analysis. Just trying to say all of that seems complicated and time consuming, but good research can ultimately have a positive influence on profits.

Start by imagining for a moment that you were to inherit a well respected company from a long lost relative. What is one of the first things you might want to know about the company? That's right; how much it is worth or how much money it makes. All of the financial documentation reported on a publicly traded company can be filtered down to a company's **market capitalization** or **Earnings per Share (EPS)**. Due to the fact that most traders are not investing, usually because of the lengthy time

> Market Capitalization – The current value of the company based on the number of existing shares multiplied by the current per share value.
>
> Earnings Per Share (EPS) – Net Profit minus Preferred Stock Dividends divided by the average outstanding shares.

commitment, short-term traders only want to know if the stock has a reason to increase or decrease in the near future.

Now, going back to the newly inherited company, if the earnings of the company are increasing and are currently positive, wouldn't you want to sell at a high price or look forward to the value increasing in the near future? The very fact that earnings are increasing suggests not only that the stock has value but that it could continue to increase. Earnings alone are not the final view of the company, however.

Reported Earnings

	03/20XX	12/20XX	09/20XX	06/20XX	
Reported	0.29	0.21	0.24	0.19	0.19
Estimate	0.25	0.21	0.21	0.19	0.16
Difference	0.04	0.00	0.03	0.00	0.03
Surprise	16.00%	0.00%	14.29%	0.00%	18.75%

Figure 1.1 Example of quarterly earnings stated as a per share amount.

Since our stock trading neighbor has suggested the purchase of a specific stock, let's take a look at the major share holders and the number of shares they hold in the company. The majority investors in the stock markets are referred to as the institutional investors. Institutional Investors include financial establishments to whom many of us are already

Institutions – Include organizations that pull monies from various private investors through mutual funds, pension funds, hedge funds, or insurance plans and together have a large influence on an individual security. The Institutional Owners are generally referred to as the *Big Money.*

giving our money. **Institutions** include banks, pension plans, mutual funds, insurance companies and others.

Think of the amount of money some of the larger insurance companies must have. If they invested a large portion of their money in a single stock, they could have a big influence on the price of the stock, due to the laws of supply and demand. This fact alone is reason enough to track the influence of institutional ownership. If the institutions are invested at a high percentage of the outstanding shares, then we like the stock because they will increase the price as they continue to buy. However, because they own a large portion of the shares, they can also affect the stock price negatively if they sell off their shares in large quantities over a short period of time.

> Liquidity – The degree at which a security can be bought or sold. The more liquid a security, the easier it is to buy or sell. Typically a stock that generates high trading volume is considered to be more liquid. The less liquid a security, the more difficult it is to buy or sell and is represented by low levels of trading volume.

On the other hand, if they own very little of the stock, we as small traders can become a driving force of the stock price movement and increase our risk of owning the stock due to the lack of **liquidity**.

The ideal situation for small or retail traders is for institutional investors to own enough but not too much. What is this vague area? This middle section will vary from company to company but should fall between 35-75% of the outstanding shares.

Institutional Shares Bought	342,468,465
Institutional Shares Sold	293,713,507
Shares Held by Institutions	6,276,161,448
# Institutions Holding Shares	2,142
% Outstanding Shares Held by Institutions	58

Figure 1.2 Example of a typical breakdown screen showing the institutional influence.

Institutional ownership is a valuable piece of fundamental information about a company. Taking the idea a step further, consider the sentiment or attitude of the institutions. Look at their ownership on a quarterly basis. Are they buying more or selling more? More is the key here. Because institutions are in the business of trying to make money, they are constantly buying and selling shares. What they are doing more of is the determining factor as to the sentiment of the institutions. Looking at whether the institutional influence increases or decreases from quarter to quarter should give you an idea of where the *big money* is moving.

Institutional money is referred to as the *big money* because of the large amounts of money the institutions trade at any given time on a single stock. To give a better visual comparison of a trader versus and institutional investor, consider a school bus and a compact car. The bus, or the institutional investor, drives to the end of a cul-de-sac and attempts a 21-point turn around. When the institution is finished and starts in the other direction, a great deal of horsepower is required to build up the momentum and drive the bus down the street in the opposite direction. The opposite is true with our compact car, the retail trader. While driving behind the slow-turning bus, it can quickly complete a 3-point turn and rush ahead of the bus out of the cul-de-sac.

If there is ever a question as to where the bus is and if it is possibly slowing for a potential reversal, the signals begin to show up in the news. Next to price movement, the news is the most current reflection of the company even though it remains a lagging indicator. The two go hand in hand. Good news will cause traders to make trades which increase the price. Bad news is just the opposite and is also represented by an increase in volume, but this volume is generated from the selling which will drive the price down.

None of us are experts on predicting the future and the news is not a crystal ball. The news simply gives us a window to the professionals that spend their days tracking and evaluating the company and the company-produced hype to interest other prospective buyers. News can often be misleading. Take for instance a news release that reports the Chief Executive Officer (CEO) of 15 years is being released. Is this good, bad or insignificant news? If you answered, *It depends*, you are correct. It depends on the company performance during this individual's tenure and how much the investors feel the CEO influenced this success. Shortly after, we can seek confirmation of the sentiment by how the stock price reacts to the news. The price may increase or decrease due to the departure of a CEO because unfortunately not all CEOs are loved by their companies and may very well be released with great fanfare from the employees and investors alike.

The ability to determine whether news is significant will develop through your history of tracking and trading the stock. Take for instance a pharmaceutical company that is looking to introduce a new drug that treats a highly publicized and widespread illness such as HIV/AIDS. The announcement of the production of this new drug could cause the price to increase. If you missed this increase, you have not necessarily missed all that this stock potentially has to offer in trades. The drug must go through development and then a strict approval process before the company can even begin to show the gains in revenue to the bottom line or earnings. Currently the movement is nothing more than early bird speculation. As the company passes the different stages of FDA approval and comes closer to the actual release date, the news announcements could produce separate short-term but valuable trade execution opportunities.

The news announcement today may be the trade opportunity of the future. Recently a pharmaceutical company released a long awaited drug for public consumption. At the time of its release announcement, the company also announced the completed development of another drug, and expected the phase 3 approvals to be completed in 12 months. This is a perfect example of valuable news that will often times be forgotten because of the time in which it was released. Many traders and investors alike will be focused on the importance of the news article as to how it relates to the current situation. In all actuality, this has produced a wonderful opportunity to be ahead of the next news trade as the FDA approval stages for the newer drug are being completed during the following year or years.

Watching the price of a stock over an extended period of time is a secondhand view of the fundamental analysis and how the analysis is being considered by the long-term investor in the marketplace. As the balance sheets, news announcements and institutional investors have taken their toll on the price of the stock, it has created an identifiable direction on the charts. Even though the chart reading will be used more for the entry and exit of the trades during the technical analysis, it also allows us to work within the confines of one of the basic fundamental evaluations: trading with the trend.

The saying *the trend is your friend* is found in nearly every investing and trading instructional material. The trend gives insight into the market community's perception of the company found in the price movement. Evaluating the trend can be one of the easiest steps in the fundamental evaluation process.

Start by deciding if you want to trade or invest in the stock. Trading refers to holding a position in the stock for a short period of time, while investing is more of a buy and hold strategy. Look at the chart of the stock and determine if the price has increased, decreased or remained relatively neutral over the evaluated time period. If investing in the stock, look at the 1-year chart. The far left price on the chart becomes point *A* and the far right price becomes point *B*. Connect the two points. If the line is increasing from left to right the trend is increasing, if the line is decreasing from left to right the trend is decreasing and if the line remains relatively flat the trend is neutral.

If you are considering the stock for trading strategies, the time frame that you evaluate should reflect twice the length of time of the expected trade duration. For example, if the expected trade move from entry price to the target price is determined to take 3 weeks, then the trend is based on a minimum of the last 6 weeks. A longer evaluation period will always give a better indication of the trend, while a shorter time frame can involve more risk due to not being as accurate to the overall trend of the stock.

> Bullish Market – Refers to the overall consensus of the stock, option, bond, or currency markets where the majority of the securities within are currently increasing, projected to increase, or expected to continue a price increase over time.
>
> Bearish Market – The direct opposite of a Bullish Market.

To complete this fundamental analysis of the stock, with a possible trade as the end result, we not only want a stock heading in the direction that we intend to trade (up trend for a **Bullish** strategy or down trend for a **Bearish** strategy), but we want the overall market and/or sector to be heading in the same direction as well. Then use the same trend evaluation process which was used for the stock on the stock's specific sector, such as the Retail Sector or Utilities Sector.

Figure 1.3 Trend evaluation of stock shows an up-trending stock.

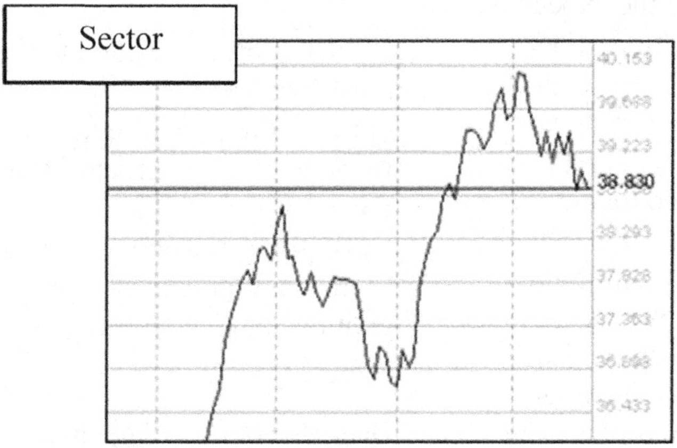

Figure 1.4 Trend evaluation of the NASDAQ market shows an up-trending market.

Price Bar – A visual representation of price movement during a single period of time. Four price points are used to create a price bar: High, Low, Open, and Close.

The purpose of completing this extra step is to reduce risk through the association of the stock and the market and/or sector. The likelihood of a stock price to continue in a given direction is only increased if the market and/or sector are moving in that same direction.

Parents often want their children to avoid associating with individuals who have a bad reputation, as guilt by association is difficult to overcome. This also holds true in the marketplace. It is not impossible for a stock price to increase when it belongs to a sector that is not increasing as a unit, but it is more difficult.

Candlestick – A visual representation of price movement during a single period of time designed to more quickly determine an increase or decrease in price during the single period of time. Each candlestick has a body (A box created by the open and closing price, where the top of the body represents either the open price (light colored box) or closing price (dark colored box).

Once you've done the first portion of the research (step two of the three-step process) is now complete. The next portion is the technical analysis within 'Research' to determine entry and exit evaluation. Technical analysis is a broad evaluation of charts, patterns, indicators and their association with one another. This can be a time-consuming process; therefore trading information websites include easy-to-read technical indicators which reduce the effort necessary to become proficient.

The chart of the stock

represents any change in price over a given period of time (usually one year or 6 months). A **price bar** or **candlestick** can depict the opening and closing, as well as the high and low prices reached in a given day. Following is an example of the basic candlestick and price bar as found on the technical price charts to reflect the price movement over many time frames.

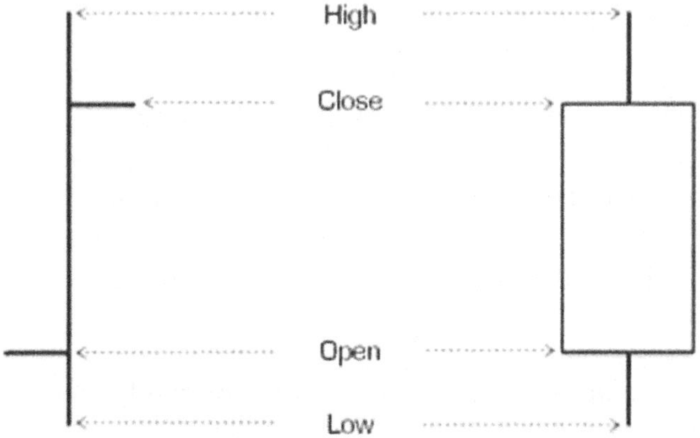

Figure 1.5 Increasing time period comparison of a Candlestick vs. Price Bar

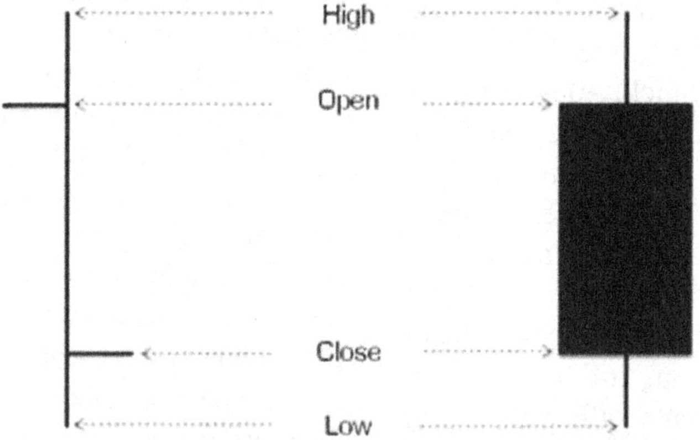

Figure 1.6 Decreasing time period comparison of a Candlestick vs. Price Bar

Basic technical analysis is completed by interpreting indicators derived from fluctuations of price, time and trading volume to better understand the price changes of a stock or option. The first and most commonly used technical indicator is the Simple Moving Average (SMA or MA). This is one of the most important tools to use. The moving average is calculated by adding up the closing prices of the previous periods that make up your specific moving average, divided by those number of time periods. It should be noted that the moving averages' time period can be made up of any given amount of time such as 30 days, 21 days, or even 5 days. As part of an entry and/or exit of a stock play, the 30-day moving average signals a bullish buy as the price crosses from below the moving average line, while the bullish sell point is when the price crosses the moving average line from above.

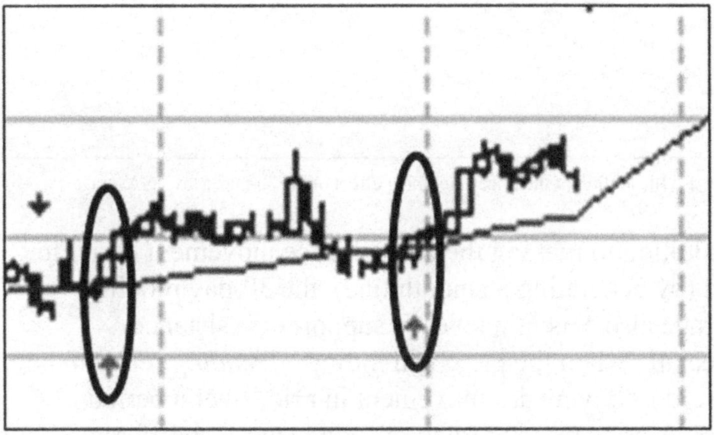

Figure 1.7 Candlestick crossing from below to above 30-Day Moving Average.

The Moving Average is a valuable tool used as one of the buy or sell indicators as well as a visual tool used to identify the price trend (Bullish or Bearish) to make sure you are trading with the trend. If the Moving Average is heading in an upward direction (as seen in Fig. 1.7), this indicates a short-term Bullish trend. A Bearish short-term price trend is identified when the Moving Average is heading downward.

Many online brokerage charting tools or other charting websites have the ability to add this indicator if it is not a default. Most charting tools will also enable you to change the time period reflected by the moving average, such as 30, 21, or 10 days. As part of the fundamental analysis, this 30-day moving average (30 MA) can be used to determine if the trend is up, down or sideways.

Figure 1.8 Illustration of the price smoothing effect of the 30-Day Moving Average.

In addition to making the overall price movement easier to read (by generating a smooth line), the 30-day moving average also acts as a level of support or resistance, especially when the price is trending. *Trending* refers to an upward or downward movement in price over a period of time. A price moving relatively sideways is a different process which will be discussed in *Trading Strategies*.

Determining levels of support and resistance is key when identifying an entry or exit point. **Support** is defined as the area in which the price slows, stops or reverses direction from a downward trend. Conversely, **resistance** refers to when the price slows, stops or reverses direction from an upward trend. In other words, support acts as a floor and resistance acts as a ceiling for price. The 30-day moving average can refer to either the floor or the ceiling depending on where it is in reference to the current price. For example, if the trend is heading down and the current price is below the 30 MA, then the 30 MA is a point of resistance. However, once the price passes the 30 MA, it now becomes a new level of support. Remember that old support becomes new resistance and old resistance becomes new support.

To further describe support and resistance, consider a bouncy super ball which can be purchased in a coin operated machine on your way out of the local grocery store. While standing in the center of the living room of a house that has a basement and a second story, imagine throwing the ball as hard as you can directly at the floor beneath you. What happens to the ball? That's right; it bounces straight up to the ceiling and quickly back down to the floor, to the ceiling and back to the floor again. It will repeat this process until it runs out of energy. The floor and ceiling of the room act as levels of support and resistance. Now imagine there is a weak spot in the ceiling of the room. Throw the ball as hard as you did the last time directly at the floor. When the ball bounces up to the ceiling (the resistance), the ball breaks through the ceiling to the second floor. Once on the second floor, the ball has all new reference points of support and resistance. The ceiling that was above the ball is now the floor beneath it, creating a new level of support. Is it possible for the ball to break back down through the weak spot in the second level? Absolutely! The new question is *what causes the price to break through these points of support or resistance?*

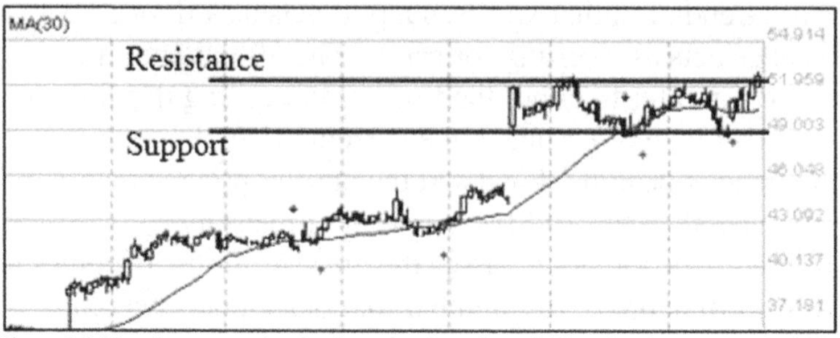

Figure 1.9 Showing current levels of support (just above $49) and resistance (nearly $62).

The answer comes from evaluating the final indicators that illustrate momentum, sentiment and volume. **Momentum** is defined as the strength or pressure being exerted behind the directional movement of the stock price. Several technical indicators are used to represent momentum. The most widely used is the Moving Average Convergence Divergence (MACD). The MACD is determined by the relationship of two separate moving averages and is represented in an easy to read histogram. As the two moving averages (12 MA and 26 MA) are calculated, they will cross one another, suggesting a buy or sell signal. A histogram is used to simplify this indicator. The crossing of the two lines is indicated when the bars of the histogram change from above to below the centerline. The online charting tools will generally allow this indicator to be added to the chart with pre-determined averages and colors. Both of which can be customized to match your trading time frame or interest.

To better demonstrate the MACD consider the unfortunate situation of having a car stuck in a snow filled ditch. To remove the car from the snow three large men stop to assist by pushing from the back of the car. Their assistance offers a level of momentum in a specific direction that if in the correct direction will result in the car being dislodged from the snow filled ditch. The situation could be made different if only one person stopped to push or if they were pushing in the opposite direction. This is the type of momentum represented on the MACD Histogram. A large histogram bar above the centerline represents the momentum of the three men pushing the car in the desired direction. A small histogram bar above the centerline is representative of the single person pushing the car from the snow filled ditch. The histogram bars on the opposite side of the centerline would be representing the men pushing from the front of the car back into the ditch. The MACD is best used to support the current price movement found on the price chart. If the price is currently increasing and the MACD is above the center line and the histogram bars are getting larger, then the indicator is suggesting the momentum is increasing in support of the price movement. This would be like the car being pushed out of the ditch with more and more people helping to push in the desired direction.

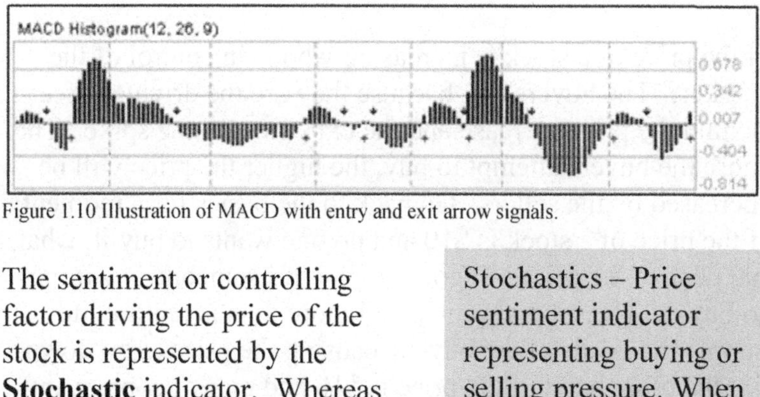

Figure 1.10 Illustration of MACD with entry and exit arrow signals.

The sentiment or controlling factor driving the price of the stock is represented by the **Stochastic** indicator. Whereas the momentum shown in the MACD dealt with the strength of the push (the number of people pushing), the Stochastic indicator shows more of the direction

Stochastics – Price sentiment indicator representing buying or selling pressure. When both moving average lines are above 80% it is considered Overbought, below 20% it is considered Oversold.

based on buying pressure and selling pressure (if the people are pushing from the front or the back of the car). It is represented in a two-line format to better show the subtle changes that can be taken advantage of as a trader.

The Stochastic indicator is a representation of the impact that buyers or sellers have on the direction of the stock. It is essentially a visual indicator of the supply and demand of the stock.

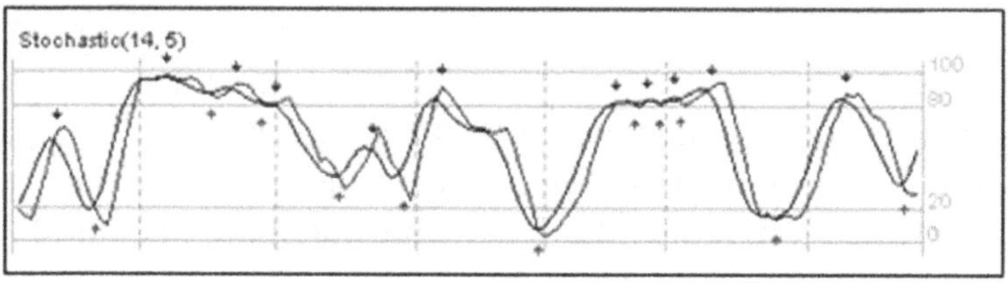

Figure 1.11 Illustration of 2-line Stochastic with entry and exit arrow signals.

If the price of a stock is increasing who is in control of the market? The buyers are, because they are the driving force behind the price increase and the extreme volume spike. The more the buyers attempt to buy, the higher the price will be increased by the sellers. Go back to the basics for a moment; if the price of a stock is $10 and no one wants to buy it, what happens to the price? It goes down until someone is willing to buy it. The sellers want to sell more than is required to supply the needs of the buyers, causing the price to go down. On the other hand, if the price is $10 and many people want to buy, what will happen to the price? The price will increase because the supply cannot meet the demand requirements. Those individuals or institutions will continue to raise the price until the supply and demand come in line with one another.

The final indicator used during the technical analysis is the volume. **Volume** is often the trump card in the analysis, because it can be as deceiving as it is helpful. Because it is so subjective, there are no red or green arrows to indicate volume. It is used more as a confirmation than an actual indicator.

Volume – A number representing the total shares traded during a given period of time.

Volume can be compared to voting. Voting is the ultimate sign of support for a cause. If a new company enters into the stock exchange, they need someone to show support for their business plan by voting *Yes*. They vote *Yes* with the almighty dollar when they buy shares of the stock. In other words, a large volume indicates lots of *Yes* votes.

Volume can be a deceptive indication however. It is often said that significant volume is needed to be an indication of a move in the stock. The question is *what is significant volume?* Significant volume is unique to each and every stock. Larger companies generally trade more volume on a given day. If the stock's trading volume (referred to as the average volume) is in the millions each day how much more is needed to be considered significant?

The higher the average volume, the less likely a large jump in the number of shares is expected or even possible in some cases. Take for instance a stock that has 10 million outstanding shares. If the average daily volume is 5 million shares (half of the total), the increase to 7.5 million would mean the stock would have to turn over three quarters of the shares on a given day. This is not impossible, but is much less likely and would certainly be a significant amount of volume. On the other hand, 6 million shares could be significant to this particular stock, and could signal a buy or sell point as the price and other indicators suggest.

In addition to examining the number of shares, consider also the consistency of the volume. If the volume is consistently between 4 and 6 million shares it only needs to move slightly above or below to be considered significant. On the opposite side of the spectrum, if the volume is less stable from one day to the next, a larger variation is necessary to be considered significant.

A good rule of thumb is that 150% of the average volume can be considered significant. Remember that the volume should always be compared to the average volume, the consistency over a period of time, the outstanding shares of the company and the actual stock itself.

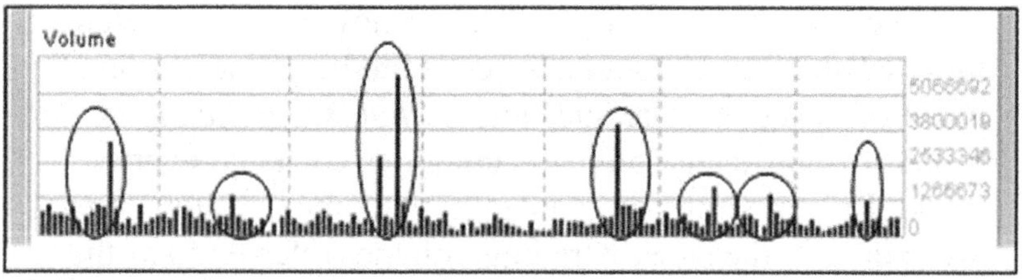

Figure 1.12 Illustration of Volume with significant volume days circled.

Step 3: Manage

Management is the tool used to get toward perfection. Because perfection is the goal of every trader and investor alike, how does one obtain perfection? Knowledge and experience are two key elements used when striving for perfection.

Step 3: This Management step is broken down into three major areas: before, during and after a trade. Before the trade, you will have obtained from the *Search* step at least one stock which you plan to trade. This stock will then be placed on a watch list waiting for the signal to begin trading once the research is completed. As the stock is traded it should be entered into the portfolio of active positions. Once the signals or standing orders require an exit of the traded position, the stock is then moved into the watch list once again, awaiting the next possible trade. Stocks can be compared to the likes of race horses; you want to race them over and over until the horse no longer performs as expected. The race horse is not good for merely one race, then left to pasture. With the amount of time and effort which has gone into locating, working with, and housing this horse you want to continue to profit from the success as long possible.

When comparing a stock to a race horse, remember, just as you would not disregard the horse after the successful race, you should not eliminate a stock after you have traded it successfully. Escort the stock back into the stables (Watch List) with the other race horses ready for the next race that fits their specific specialties for success.

The final area within the management step is practicing your strategy, as done in *Paper Trading*. The **paper trading** process is used as an actual trading account and should be used to simulate trades to better understand the effectiveness of your trading habits before applying actual dollars. The *Paper Trade process* can be utilized for testing new strategies, trading guidelines or searching results. For instance, if a search technique returns 25 results, you could paper trade all 25 results to find their statistical return. Doing this will help you better evaluate the search parameters. If 40% of the results of a search eventually produce winners, and, each of those *winners* generates 20% more profit than the 60% lost by the *losers*, than you have the start of a possible system. The search can be tested in

> Paper Trading – The process of trading stocks, options, mutual funds, ETFs, and indices with current market data but within a fictional account.

different market conditions and compared to earlier results to see if changes in the market affect the results.

Ultimately, the 3-Step Process (Step 1: Search, Step 2: Research, and Step 3: Manage) will enable you to remain focused on your trading objectives yet be more profitable by removing the emotions. If you are to alter any part of the process within a step, such as within Step 1: Search, make one or two guideline alterations and test the impact. It is difficult to understand the influence the changes will make to a system over time if you change too many components simultaneously.

As an example, let us assume you have traded the top 3 stocks returned from a search with a 15% profit in an average of 19 days. If the criteria of your search included locating only stocks with a price between $15 and $25, Average Daily Volume of 1 million shares or more, a Reward/Risk Ratio of 3:1 comparing the current price to Resistance and Support levels, as well as one that pays dividends and you changed all the criteria at once, it will be difficult to know what modification had the greatest influence toward positive or negative returns once you begin trading the new search results. Instead, perhaps modify the price range from $15 to $25 to something above this such as $25 to $40. This will allow you to see how sensitive your system is to price which will allow for a quicker response to a news tip of the *hot stock* that is priced above where you have found success previously.

A big part of the *Manage* step is to manage your emotions before, during, and after the trade. Don't allow an outside source to blindly influence your proven process of success. Take all suggestions, advice, or tips and place them into your system and if a trade is triggered and meets your criteria, excellent, make the trade. If not, don't make the trade, have no regrets, and sleep well.

Successful trading is the result of proper execution of a well designed and tested process; otherwise it would be little more than gambling or simply guesswork. Trading in the stock and option markets is a profession that can be compared to many other professions in the sense that following a proven process brings an expected result. Consider the carpenter who is most effective by having the design and plans to the home before starting to build. The carpenter follows the plans previously created with few alterations toward the expected result of a home with precise measurements, room locations, doors that open and close, as well as many other working features. The carpenter could certainly build a home from memory and past experience but the chance of error increases, the likelihood of additional costs are high, and the final result may be quite different than originally imagined. Have a plan and manage the plan toward predictable cash flow profits.

Chapter 2

Trading With an Understanding of Risk

Wanting to place a trade using this 3-Step process is understandable. But before you run out and place your first trade under the system you must evaluate and understand risk. Risk is defined by how much you are willing to lose to be right or profitable. It is certainly more than someone living dangerously (base jumping into an unknown sinkhole in the middle of the jungle), or the opposite, being extremely cautious (limiting all jumping activities to hopscotch in the park).

The described risk can be found in every trade, only in varying amounts. For example, assume you have purchased a stock, Example Inc (EXPL) for $25. The technical analysis suggests an up-trending (Bullish) stock with a price resistance level (price ceiling) at $28 and a price support level (price floor) at $24. At this point, the risk of the trade is the amount invested in the stock of $25 due to the fact that it is possible the stock price can go to zero and bring your value to zero along with the price drop.

In the world of trading and investing, **risk** equates to dollars and cents. It is the amount one is willing to lose in an effort to be profitable. Risk is a calculated comparison of the potential rewards and losses. Without an understanding of risk and how it applies to trading, you are going blindly into the markets. Yes, every once in a while a blind squirrel finds a nut, but this is no way to live and enjoy retirement. Understanding what risk you are willing to accept is important in trading and striving for successful and repeatable returns.

There are different types of risk to consider, such as trade risk and portfolio risk. **Portfolio risk** refers to how much of your entire portfolio capital you want to risk in a specific trade. For example, if a $10,000 account was spread out in at least two positions, roughly $5,000 will be allotted to each trade. **Trade risk**, on the other hand, deals with how much risk is allowed for a single position and takes into account the parameters of the stock itself.

Portfolio risk is determined by the accuracy of your previous trade decisions and will be illustrated more clearly by expectancy ratios that will be discussed shortly. Ultimately, the better your decision making process, (the more times you select a winning trade versus a losing trade), the fewer positions you will need to be in at one time while maintaining a manageable risk level through proper portfolio diversification. A quick example of a diversified portfolio is one that has equal amounts of money invested in technology companies, agricultural companies, and consumer goods companies.

Trade risk is the amount you are willing to lose to generate an expected return within a single trade; not to suggest you ever want to lose anything, but remember *it takes money to make money* certainly applies. This is due mainly to the fact that not every trade placed will be a winner. Therefore, portfolio and trade risk become a set of rules and parameters to limit losses when a trade is flawed which limits your risk. To set risk parameters consider items such as the price of the stock, the support and resistance levels and the reward/risk ratio (R/R Ratio) to be used (or a stop loss percentage).

Using a **Reward/Risk Ratio** or a stop loss percentage can make a large difference in the number of shares you purchase, or in the amount of risk you are willing to expose your account to in a single trade. A stop loss percentage is a personal amount used to identify at what point or price the trade

Reward/Risk Ratio – The ratio of the amount projected to earn as a reward if the trade is completed as projected compared to the amount being allowed or willing to lose if the trade goes against the projections.

must be exited to remove yourself and the trade from any further risk. A standard rule of thumb published throughout the market place is a 10% entry stop loss amount. This refers to allowing no more than a price reversal of 10% of the purchase price. For example, if a stock was purchased at $50, then the stop loss order, using a 10% rule, would be set at $45.

A more detailed approach to calculating how much you are willing to risk in an individual trade is the reward/risk ratio (R/R Ratio), which is how much you project to earn compared to the amount you are willing to lose if incorrect. This method of establishing the exit price takes into account the price of the stock when purchased along with support or resistance price levels and how often you are correct.

To calculate a Reward/Risk Ratio, start by calculating how many times the trades placed are profitable and how many are not profitable. Simply add up the total number of winning trades placed in an account (paper or real), then divide by the number of losing trades (bought and then sold).

$$\frac{\text{Profitable Trades}}{\text{Losing Trades}} = \frac{\text{75 (of 100)}}{\text{25 (of 100)}} = \text{3:1 R/R Ratio}$$

Until a winner versus a loser ratio is established, a basic 2:1 R/R Ratio will be used to simplify the process. This 2:1 ratio dictates that for every dollar risked, two dollars of potential reward must be available.

Apply the 2:1 ratio to the potential of the stock. Identify the support and resistance price levels. In the case of an up-trending (Bullish) stock, the price ceiling (Resistance) level will also be the target exit price.

Figure 2.1 Identifying Support and Resistance

In Fig 2.1 the support level is $49 and the resistance level is slightly above $51. Assume the purchase price is $49.75. The identified target price of $51 is an increase of $1.25 from the purchase price of $49.75. To complete the R/R Ratio stop loss amount, apply the 2:1 ratio to the $1.25. ($1.25/2 = $0.625) Subtract the ratio amount from the purchase price to maintain the required ratio, which would be $49.125. This is quit a bit different than the earlier $45 determined from the straight 10% stop loss approach. Remember, both are correct, but they each use a different approach to managing your trades. You will want to use the R/R Ratio approach when you have established a reasonable amount of trade history (25 or more trades within a specific set of trading rules or trading strategy). The percent stop-loss approach is used when you find it difficult to identify price support (floor) and price resistance (ceiling) levels. The 10% rule of thumb is also a conservative amount which is used because of the unknowns (Support and Resistance levels).

Risk can be a scary word when it comes to trading but it certainly does not need to be. For many, risk equates to larger profit potential due to the fact that the higher the perceived risk means the more potential loss is generally offset by a greater amount of potential profit. Unfortunately, that is not always the case and is one of the reasons many traders lose a great deal of money when they are just starting out. Not having risk guidelines, such as a stop-loss amount, means not having a complete trading strategy that is repeatable and therefore used for consistent, predictable profits.

Chapter 3

The Lifecycle of a Trade

The cycle of a trade using a 3-Step Investing Process can be applied immediately. In the following example you will be taken step by step through an actual trade using a 3-Step Investing Process.

Step 1: Search

Newspapers, radio talk shows and investing cable television shows are bursting with ideas of stocks to trade. With such a large number of possibilities, how can anyone go wrong by buying all of them? It would be foolish to think you could apply your strategy to all of the stocks suggested from multiple sources. Your first step in the research process is to make sure you are aware of what you are seeking. Once you have a bit of experience under your belt, you will be able to quickly take the number of guru recommendations, website suggestions, financial advisor suggestions, or any other tool that provides a list of potential stocks to trade and prepare to apply Step 2. Each may very well be a great trade if the correct strategy is applied, it just may not be what you have planned based on your risk, capital and time frame to trade. Keep in mind all of the resources mentioned are ways to gather current or potential Trades. What makes them great trades are when the proper stocks meeting your search criteria are passed along to *Step 2: Research;* then, when triggered for a trade, you act by properly trading then managing the transaction.

Step 2: Research

Once you've chosen a stock obtained from the search, it must now be run through a filtering process to verify the value to us as traders. The filtering step begins by identifying the trend of the stock.

As shown in Fig 3.2, the current trend over the last month is *up* (Draw a line from the closing price one month ago to the current closing price. As shown in Fig. 3.2, an upward pointing line identifies the uptrend.) Since we want to buy the stock with as little risk as possible, we look for an up-trending stock.

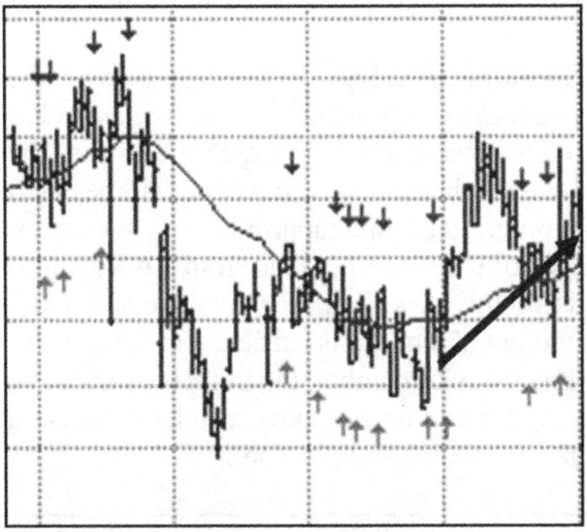

Figure 3.2 Stock chart used to evaluate the trend as part of the fundamental evaluation in the Research step.

Exchange Traded Fund (ETF) – A security that trades like a stock and experiences price changes throughout the trading day as a result of buying and selling. The ETF tracks the movement of a corresponding index, commodity, or group of diversified securities.

To further our understanding of the stock's trend, we compare the stock to the sector or market that it belongs to. In the case of *Proctor and Gamble*, which is traded on the New York Stock Exchange, we will look at identifying the trend of an **Exchange Traded Fund (ETF)** which reflects the overall performance of large value stocks on the NYSE. Two heavily traded securities can be selected in this case; the Diamond (DIA) or the SPX. The Diamond is based on the Dow Jones Industrial 30 stocks, where the SPX reflects the S&P 500. For our comparison, we will use the S&P 500 (a collection of the 500 largest revenue producing companies in the stock market) due to the larger pool of stocks taken into account.

In the chart of the SPX, Fig 3.3, we are at a point where our trading time horizon will make a big difference in how we read this chart. Because we are expecting to trade the stock and not invest in the company, the trend will be determined from a short period of time (approximately six weeks). In the current chart of the SPX, the trend from 6 weeks ago to today shows it is slightly down to flat. Of course it would be ideal to have an uptrend, but flat is sufficient to continue the research process. (Remember, the trend is evaluated by connecting a point in time, approximately six weeks ago, to the current time with a straight line.)

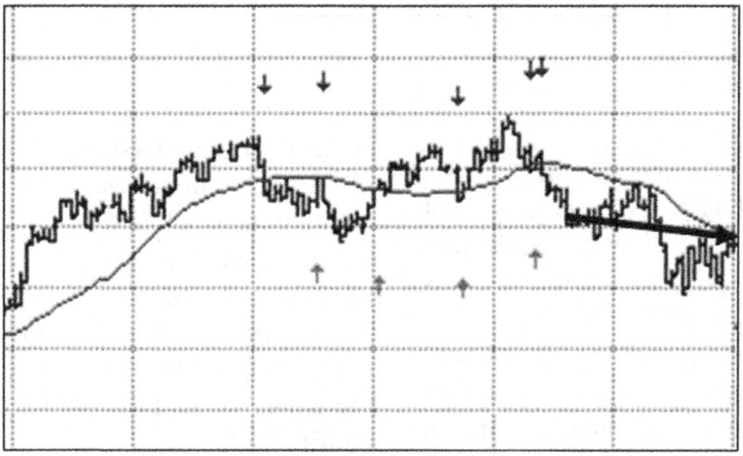

Figure 3.3 Stock chart used to evaluate the timing and potential of the possible trade.

Earnings are the next evaluation filter. Evaluation of a company based on their earnings is a good start, but it can also be deceiving, and is therefore not the only criteria. At the very least, the earnings of the company should be positive. A company operating at a loss can only stay in business for so long. In addition to positive earnings, we also want to see stabilized earnings from quarter to quarter, or, ideally, increased earnings. For a short-term trade, the understanding gained by a long-term view of the company is not worth the time it takes. Therefore, we want to evaluate the last 3 changes in the quarterly earnings.

As seen in Fig 3.4 the first quarter represented is March of 20xx. This is the benchmark to work from. The first quarter shows a decrease, followed by increases in the next two quarters. A market wide rule of thumb requirement is that at least two out of three quarters increase or remain the same. Unfortunately, these results do not meet the criteria, as the first quarter showed a loss. However, in the quarter that did not increase, the company did beat estimates, which does add to the value of the quarter because at least they did better than expected by the analysts.

Reported Earnings

	12/20XX	09/20XX	06/20XX	03/20XX
Reported	0.74	0.73	0.50	0.55
Estimate	0.71	0.71	0.48	0.54
Difference	0.03	0.02	0.02	0.01
Surprise	4.23%	2.82%	4.17%	0.93%

Figure 3.4 Stock earnings reported used in the evaluation of the fundamental evaluation in the Research step.

Institutional ownership of this company can make or break the evaluation. The institutions spend plenty of time and money to acquire the most current and reliable information on the company's projections in earnings, market share, new products and supply and demand. They then use this information to buy, sell or hold positions in the company to ultimately make the investments back and turn a profit from the future value of the stock price.

The drawback for institutions is the time it takes for a large number of shares to be bought or sold in the market place. Many institutions have teams of individuals that trade only a small variety of stocks, placing trades that may take days to fill orders of buy or sell. This turns into an advantage for the retail investor because we are generally not going to buy or sell millions of dollars worth of a stock in a given order allowing us to be quicker and more nimble with our trades. We therefore turn to the number of institutions with the outstanding shares, and the buying or selling pressure that the institutions collectively have on the stock.

On many trading tool websites, the influence of institutions is easy to read and allows a quick filter of this information to determine whether the influence is good, bad or neutral. In Fig 3.5 we see that the institutions have purchased 40 million more shares than they sold over the recent three month time period. If institutions are buying more than they are selling, what is likely to happen to the price? The price will increase to match the demand the institutions are creating by buying more than they are selling.

In addition to knowing whether the institutions are buying more than they are selling, it is equally important to know how much of an influence the institutions have on the outstanding shares. This is represented by the *Percent Outstanding Shares Held by Institutions*. The desired amount of institutional influence in a trading strategy should ideally be between 35% and 75%.

Institutional Holdings	2005/06
Institutional Shares Bought	132,241,543
Institutional Shares Sold	92,149,280
Shares Held by Institutions	1,510,008,623
# Institutions Holding Shares	1,710
% Outstanding Shares Held by Institutions	61

Figure 3.5 Snapshot of Institutional ownership found on the company being evaluated.

The ownership percentage determines how much control the institutions have on the price. If they own too little (less than 35%), the retail investors become an active player in the movement in the price of the stock which means liquidity is low. If liquidity is low, the risk of loss in the stock's value increases, making it difficult to capture the value created by the market because you have become the market influence. If the institutions own more than 75%, they can be considered to have too much control. As a trader understands the influence of the institutions, the trade will be observed more closely and perhaps even in a shorter time frame than usual.

Evaluating the news is the final step in our fundamental analysis of the stock. Next to the actual price movements, the news is the most current reflection of the stock, and is a window into the company and its investors. It is important to note that the news we read is more times than not paid PR from the company. Therefore the news article will be on positive information or have a positive twist to what could be negative situations. To try and reduce the influence of paid-for news articles consider the source. If the news is covered by multiple news firms such as CNN, CNBC, MSNBC, Reuters, or Businessweek it is less likely to have been paid publicity. In addition, many times the source will simply state that it is a paid advertisement or press release which suggests it is coming straight from the company itself.

The news will be used by the trader to verify the significance of the price moves. Looking at the news article in Fig 3.6, decide if it is good news, bad news or neither. Look for the price to increase if it is good news, decrease if it is bad news, or do very little of anything if the news is neutral.

> Proctor & Gamble Co., the nation's largest household products maker, said Thursday that fiscal third-quarter earnings rose 13 percent, driven by volume increases across all business units that were partially offset by continued marketing investments.
>
> Cincinnati-based P&G reported net income of $1.72 billion, or 63 cents per share, compared with $1.53 billion, or 55 cents per share a year ago.
>
> Sales grew 10 percent to $14.29 billion from $13.03 billion last year.
>
> Analysts surveyed by Thomson Financial were expecting earnings of 61 cents per share on sales of $13.91 billion in the quarter.

Figure 3.6 Stock news reported by a variety of news sources

This turns out to be great news due to the earnings beating estimates ($0.63 versus $0.61) as well as the year of year earnings increase of 13% and a revenue increase of 10%. We can now proceed to the technical analysis.

Technical analysis is the process of reading the chart to determine the potential return and the entry/exit points. To start this process, we will begin at the bottom and work our way up the chart.

Volume is the first indicator to observe. What is the average volume? What is the volume today?

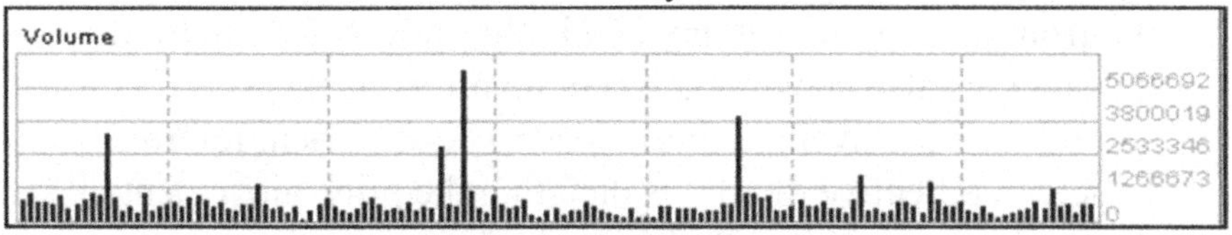

Figure 3.7 Stock volume representing the number of shares traded.

The volume is given on the right side of the chart and is broken down in increments depending on the largest volume day in the last year. The volume today is 166,900. The calculated average volume is 729,600 shares per day, which suggests the current volume is not very significant.

The Moving Average Convergence Divergence (MACD) histogram, which shows momentum like the individuals pushing you out of the snow filled ditch introduced earlier, is the next indicator to analyze. The height of the histogram above or below the center line shows the strength of the momentum in the Bullish or Bearish direction.

Looking at the most recent and current center line cross, it appears that an up pointing arrow is helping to identify the center line cross from the bottom to the top of the centerline on the MACD Histogram. The upward cross is a visual representation on many technical charting tools with an up arrow and is a Bullish trigger or indicator.

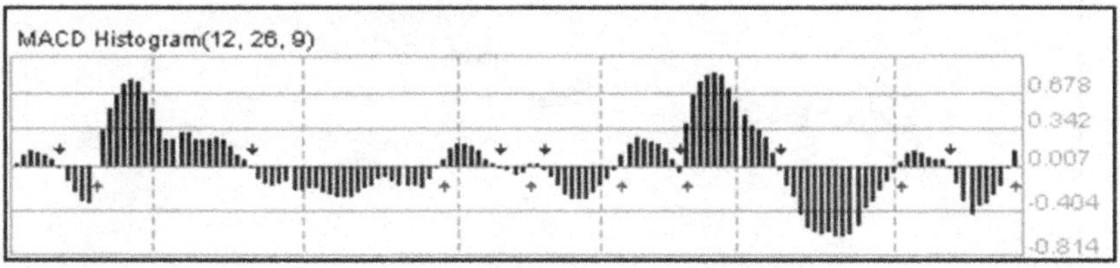

Figure 3.8 Technical indicator (MACD) used to measure momentum.

The Stochastic, which represents the sentiment (buying or selling pressure represented like the individuals pushing from the front or back of the car stuck in the snow filled ditch) of the stock, is also showing a recent up arrow as the two smooth moving average lines cross. The sentiment referred to here is reflective of who is dictating the price movement, the buyers or the sellers. The Stochastics could be considered the supply and demand curves generally discussed from an economic point of view.

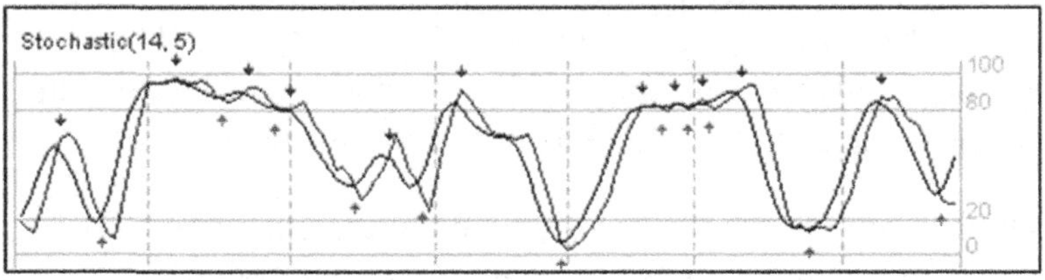

Figure 3.9 Technical indicator (Stochastic) used to measure trading sentiment.

The final signal to evaluate in determining the entry point is the price and where it crosses the 30-day moving average (MA). In this case, the stock is moving up and recently crossed the moving average (also indicated by the up arrow) suggesting a Bullish trigger or indicator.

Figure 3.10 Technical indicator (30-Day Moving Average) used to smooth the price fluctuations.

The signals found in figures 3.7, 3.8, 3.9, and 3.10 are all Bullish, but before the trade is made the potential return must also be considered. This is where determining the support and resistance prices become so valuable. In the case of this particular example, the support price is approximately $52 (the old resistance and the price recently exceeded) and the resistance price is approximately $55. The current price is $52.08, which suggests there is more up-side potential than down-side potential. The green arrows are signaling a buy of the stock, and based on the resistance level of $55.00, we have a potential return of $2.92 at our target and/or exit price of $55.00. This is only the first level of resistance. If the stock does not have red arrows, bad news, decreasing earnings, or other negative signs, there is no reason to exit the position. We would stay in the trade and more growth could occur.

The exit is just as important as the entry if we are correct, and if the trade turns and is incorrect. A stop-loss order can protect a trade from a continued loss as the price falls. As mentioned earlier, a stop-loss order will be based on either a percent or the Reward Risk Ratio. A 10% stop-loss order would be set at $46.87. Thinking through this particular trade should be alarming at this point. The potential return is $2.92 and the stop loss amount is $5.21. This is a negative risk ratio, which means we are willing to lose nearly 2 times as much as we have the potential to make. This is not a wise idea.

The Reward Risk Ratio determines the stop loss amount based on the potential return. By using the 2:1 Reward Risk Ratio, the stop-loss order will be very tight in comparison to the stop loss percentage approach, and will cause you to exit trades more frequently. The increased frequency is a bad situation if you are consistently trading stocks with too little upside potential. However, the quick unemotional reaction triggering the exit trade to the stock's negative movement will limit the losses and help you remain in control of the trades, therefore meaning that no single loss can ruin the account. The 2:1 ratio suggests that we allow for a $1.46 reversal before the trade is given up as a loss. The alternate stop loss price is $50.62.

Step 3: Manage

Trading is much easier with a plan in place much like having a map for a cross country trip. The plan is only as good as the person following the plan. This is the very reason the final step of the 3-Step Investing Process is to properly *Manage* the trade.

In the case of this particular stock we are ready to actually place the trade. If, however, the trade was not completely ready to be placed, it would be placed into a watch list to track and wait for the missing criteria to signal the trade. (An example would be waiting for the last of the three technical indicators to trigger.)

We are going to place our trade and make a record of the trade information (for example, trade date, number of shares, target price, stop-loss amount, price support and resistance levels, and current price trend) to evaluate our trading decisions.

Placing the trade is done through a broker. A typical broker order screen will have the following important features: Buy or Sell choice, the number of shares and symbol, order type and expiration of the order.

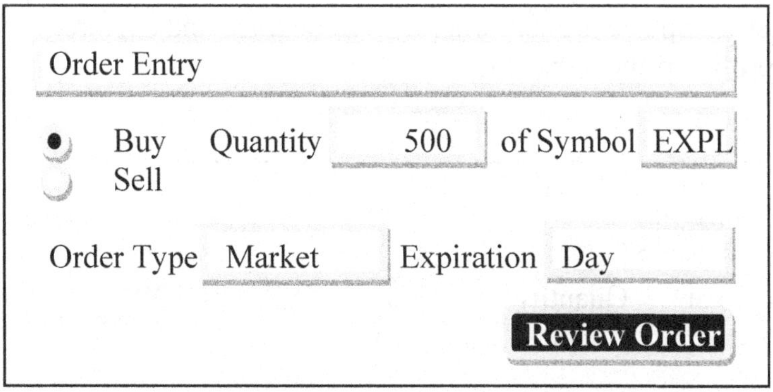

Figure 3.11 Typical order entry screen found with on-line brokers. Illustrating an entry order.

In this example, the expiration is at the end of the current market day. This means that if the order is not filled by the time the market closes today, it will expire. It is possible to have a partial fill during the day, which can be anywhere from 1 to 499 of the 500 shares requested to buy. If you only want the order to be filled if you can have all the shares requested, then add the special instruction of *All or None*.

> Day-Trader – Individual trading into and out of market security positions throughout the trading day.

Click on *Review Order*, verify the information is correct, then click *Submit Order*.

As soon as the order has been filled it will appear in the account totals and the current holdings or portfolio. During this time period of ownership, you will be able to quickly view the stock's current price performance and the impact to your account value. Due to the fact that you are not a **Day-Trader**, you will not need to watch the stock's price performance continuously.

If the stock price suddenly increases to the target price and the technical indicators are in a potential trend reversal situation, it may be time to sell. Return to the brokerage screen and place the sell order to exit the trade and capture the profits of the transaction.

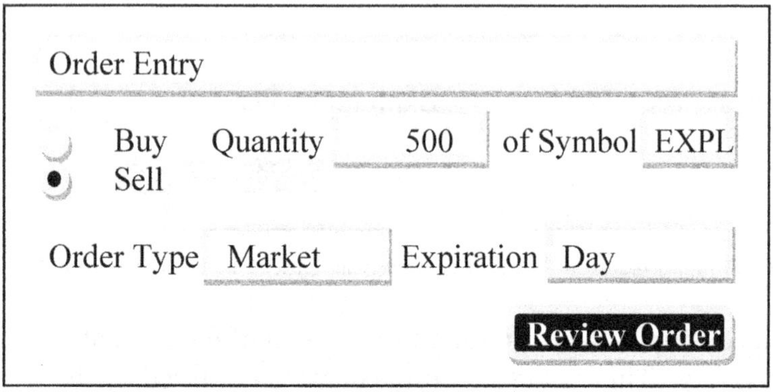

Figure 3.12 Typical order entry screen found with on-line brokers illustrating an exit order.

Although the trade is now completed, the stock is not rendered useless. At this time the stock is reentered in your watch list for future trade possibilities. Stocks can be traded multiple times throughout the course of a year or years. As long as the fundamental analysis is updated on a regular basis and the technical signals show the next signs of entry, it is time to trade!

Chapter 4

The Cash Flow Strategy

When you make any investment, there are three basic things that can happen which will impact your investment.

The three things that can happen when you invest:

1. It will go up in value
2. It will remain the same
3. It will go down in value

Most people I meet invest money with the expectation that whatever they are investing in will go up in value. I guess you could say it's the *American Way* to invest and earn a profit if it rises in value. Unfortunately, that's only one of the three possible outcomes. If the investment stays at the same value, you've not lost any money, but you will have lost opportunity because you could have been investing in something else that did increase in value. If the investment drops in value, you will suffer a loss on your investment.

So the way most invest, they have a one in three chance of making money. Those are pretty risky odds, but millions of investors successfully invest billions of dollars every single day with those odds.

The Cash Flow Strategy is a simple approach to investing that offers you an opportunity to profit in all three potential scenarios. That's what this specific cash flow strategy is all about. I'm going to teach you a simple, low-risk strategy that actually allows you to make money when a stock rises, stays the same, or even falls a little bit in price. Let's face it; it's hard to pick stocks that go up in price every single time. I've yet to meet a stock trader, even those so-called *gurus*, who don't pick losers from time to time.

This simple strategy and approach to trading can dramatically increase your chances of making a profit. It's not unusual for a trader using this approach to win nearly every trade they make, or at least 80-90%. If you hate losing money as much as I do, then this is the strategy for you.

In order for you to see the power of my first cash flow strategy, you must first have a basic understanding of options. Options are investment vehicles that allow you to participate in the stock market without really buying or selling actual stocks. It's a bit like making side bets on the stock market. I love to invest with options and they are a key part of learning to unlock the earning power of your portfolio to generate consistent monthly cash flow from your investments.

There are two basic types of options contracts

1. Put options
2. Call options

For this first cash flow strategy, we're going to focus our attention on Call Options.

A **Call option** is a contract that gives the owner the right (but not the obligation) to buy a stock at a set price, referred to as the strike price, on or before a set date in the future. Let's look at an example to make some sense of this definition.

Let's say Example, Inc stock (EXPL) is trading for around $25 per share. Based upon our research, we determine that it should move higher over the next few months. To capitalize on our forecast, we can simply buy 100 shares of EXPL at $25 per share for a total investment of $2500 and hold on to the stock in hopes of selling those shares at a higher price in the future.

Let's say we're right in our forecast and several months later EXPL is trading for $30 per share. We could sell our 100 shares of EXPL for $3000 and make a nice $500 profit on our investment. The $500 profit would amount to a 20% return on our initial investment of $2500.

That's how most people would take advantage of the opportunity they saw in EXPL, but there is another way to take advantage of it using less money, with greater potential using options.

Instead, let's say you bought the $25 call option on EXPL that expires in three months rather than buying shares. This option contract would give you the right to buy 100 shares of EXPL stock at $25 anytime until it expires in three months. In most cases you'll never actually exercise your contractual right to purchase the $100 shares of EXPL, but it's this right that ultimately determines the value of the contract you hold. To obtain the right to buy EXPL at $25 for this period time, you must buy a **Call Option contract**. These contracts are traded on several option markets around the country and the prices are clearly established and easy to find. The price of an option contract is referred to as the Premium.

Call Option Contract – A contract that gives the owner the right to buy 100 shares at the Strike price on or before the expiration date.

Let's look at an example: Let's say the EXPL $25 three-month call option is currently selling for $1.50. Options are quoted in *per share* prices. Most option contracts are based upon 100 shares of stock, so to determine the cost of the contract; you would multiply the price by 100. Using this information, you can see that the cost of the EXPL $25 call option would be $150 ($1.50 quote X 100 shares).

That's far less than the $2500 it would cost to buy 100 shares of EXPL, but you still maintain control of the same amount of stock. If you chose to invest the same number of dollars in EXPL options, you could control many times more stock for the same amount of money by using call options. That's the leverage of options. It takes less money to control a larger block of stock.

Your risk in this play is limited to the price you pay for the option. In this case your risk would be $150. That's the most you can lose, no matter what EXPL stock does between now and expiration day. Compare this to the risk of buying the 100 shares of EXPL stock. There is no rule in the stock market that says a stock can't go to zero. If you don't believe me, just ask anyone who bought Enron or any number of Internet companies that went bust when the dot com bubble burst in the 1990s. So when you buy a stock, 100% of your investment is at risk. It's the same with an option contract; except that the initial dollars invested to control a block of stock with an option contract is ALWAYS a fraction of the actual cost for the same number of shares.

Now let's fast forward to three months from now when the EXPL stock is at $30 per share. At this point the investor who owns the $25 call option can simply sell the option contract in the option market for the current price and realize their profit. This is no more complicated than selling a block of shares in the stock market. The value of the option will be based upon the difference in the *strike price* of the option, which is $25 in this example and the current price of the stock. The difference between $25 and $30 is $5. So in this example the EXPL $25 call option will be worth at least $5 per share or $500 per contract if EXPL goes to $30 per share before the option expires.

If the option investor sells the option for $500, they will have a profit of $350 after subtracting the $150 they paid for the contract. In this example the percentage return on the EXPL call option is over 100% compared with the 20% return for the stock buyer.

Initial Investment	**Value @ $30**	**Profit**	**Percentage**
Stock = $2500	$3000	$500	20%
Call Option = $150	$350	$200	133%

That's the leverage of options. A small amount of money can control a large amount of stock. Call options are a popular investment in bull markets where stocks are rising in value. Call options give an investor an opportunity to profit from the rise in value of a stock without ever actually owning the stock at all.

Trading in options has exploded over the past years as more and more investors discover the power of using options as a way to control risk and increase profit potential.

What I want you to learn is that there are no rules that say you can only buy options. In each option transaction there is a buyer and a seller. The buyer pays a premium to own the contract and the seller collects the premium in return for taking on the obligation of the contract.

The secret to unlocking the earning power of your portfolio involves learning how to use options to generate monthly income from your investments. When you own 100 shares of stock, you can sell another investor the right to buy those shares from you at a set price for a set period of time. This is accomplished by selling a call option, just like the one used in our EXPL example.

Let's look at that same transaction from the side of the call option seller to see how it worked for them.

Let's assume for this example that the seller owned at least 100 shares of MSFT when they sold the call option, which is the easiest and safest way to cover the *obligation* or risk that is associated with selling a call option. At the time they sold the call option EXPL stock was trading at $25 per share, so their 100 shares would be worth $2500. Perhaps they didn't see any reason for EXPL to rise over the next few months so they chose a strategy that would guarantee them some income from their EXPL shares regardless of what the stock does.

This strategy is called a *covered call* strategy. The 100 shares of MSFT stock the investor owns covers the obligation of the call option they sell. No matter what price EXPL goes to by the expiration day of the option, the seller will be able to fulfill the obligation to sell 100 shares because they actually own them. The price the option buyer will have to pay for the shares is determined by the *Strike Price* (contractual face value of the option contract if exercised) of the call option contract, in this case $25.

When an investor decides to sell a call option to *cover* their stock, they can choose which price from the available list of call options that they are willing to sell their stock. The lower the price (strike price) of the call option contract they select, the higher the premium they will collect.

One other aspect that will influence the price of a call option is how long until it expires. The longer the time frame of the option, the higher the premium due to the fact that every day has value based on another day of potential for the underlying stock to increase or decrease. The longer you're willing to tie up your stock, the more someone is willing to pay you for the right to buy it due to the likelihood of a price increase of the underlying stock over time.

The money you collect when you sell an option is deposited into your brokerage account the next day and is available for you to withdraw. You've just created cash flow from your stock! Don't confuse cash flow with profit. You won't know if the money you collected from the option is a profit until the option expires or you close it out prior to expiration.

In our EXPL example, the option seller would collect $1.50 per share ($150 per contract) in premiums by selling the $25 call option. This money is theirs to keep whether or not they end up having to sell their stock or not.

When you complete a covered call trade, there are two possible outcomes that will be determined by what the underlying stock does by expiration day. Let's see what each of these potential outcomes would look like in our EXPL example.

As stated earlier, there are only three things EXPL can do from here:

1. Go up in price
2. Stay the same
3. Go down in price

Let's look at each potential outcome and evaluate the results.

Stays the same or goes down in price

If EXPL is trading for any price below the strike price of the option ($25), the option will expire rendering the contract worthless. This will result in the expiration of the obligation to sell the 100 shares of EXPL that was bought by the option buyer. The option seller would get to keep their stock and the $150 in income that was generated from the covered call strategy. They would now be free to enter into another covered call play using a different call option for a future expiration month and collect another premium.

Since options expire on a monthly basis on the third Friday of each month, it's possible for a covered call trader to generate consistent monthly income from the stocks they own, provided there are options available and they own a minimum of 100 shares of the underlying stock.

I personally like to trade covered calls each month on my stock and thereby create a consistent source of income from my portfolio regardless of what the stock market is doing. It's just like getting a monthly paycheck from your invested capital.

Stock price goes up

If the stock is higher than the strike price of the call option on expiration day the stock will be **called away** from the option seller at the **strike price**. This is just like selling the stock at $25. If the option seller doesn't want to sell their EXPL stock at $25 in the first place, they would have never entered into this covered call trade. There is always the possibility of being *called away* from your stock when you're selling

Strike Price – The fixed price in the contract where a derivative can be purchased (Call) or Sold (Put) when exercised.

Called Away – The process of executing a derivative contract to buy (Call) or sell (Put) the underlying stock.

covered call options. But the magic is that you collected an extra $1.50 per share from the covered call which means you actually collected $26.50 per share, not just $25.

Profit when stock rises above your call option strike price

Strike Price + Premium = Total Selling price
$25 + $1.50 = $26.50 per share

There are two primary risks associated with the covered call strategy

1. You are subject to the same risk that anyone who owns shares would have. Your investment may lose value if the price of the shares decline while you own them. While this is a risk, it is minimized somewhat by the income that can be generated by selling a call option contract. So the covered call investor will actually have less risk than another investor who simply owns shares and doesn't use the covered call strategy.
2. Using the covered call strategy puts a limit on the potential profits you can earn from your shares. When you sell a call option contract with a specific strike price, you are agreeing to sell your shares at that price. Should the price rise higher than the strike price of your covered call option, you would not participate in that additional increase. Your maximum profit on a typical covered call play is limited to the strike price of the contract plus the premium collected.

I have to list #2 as a risk, but in reality if you ever do a covered call trade and have to sell your stock at the maximum potential profit, you've more than likely earned a profit. You may be disappointed that you didn't earn *More* profit, but it's hard to be too upset when you still made money. I call this a *too much of a good thing* situation. I can assure you that this is far better than losing money.

The process of being called out is handled automatically by the brokerage firm and requires no follow-up action by the option seller. After the normal 3-day settlement period for a stock transaction, the funds from the sale of the stock will be available in your account to invest in another trade.

When I get called out of a stock as a result of the stock rising higher than the strike price of a covered call that I've sold, I try to remember that I've made the maximum possible profit from the strategy I chose to use and ignore the possibility that I may have been able to make more money had I not done a covered call at all. All I lost was some of the opportunity. I still made a profit and that was the goal.

Now let's look at the downside of the covered call strategy so you understand the risk involved in using this approach in your investing.

If the stock should fall from the current price of $25, the option seller has $1.50 of *downside protection* in the form of the option premium income. This is like a little insurance against a dip in the price of the stock. If the stock stays below the strike price of the covered call, the call option will expire and the option seller will keep the income from the covered call and their stock.

If the stock should drop more than the $1.50 in option premium income, the option seller would begin to lose money. While selling covered calls is a great way to minimize the downside risk of owning a stock, it doesn't remove it altogether. The only sure way to remove the continued risk of owning a stock is to sell it.

Using the covered call strategy is a great way to ride out the dips that most stocks take from time to time and generate income from stocks that are not moving.

My single favorite way to use this strategy to generate income is by applying the covered call strategy to the QQQ, the exchange traded fund that follows the Nasdaq 100 index. This is a very liquid market for both stock and options and a great place to learn this strategy. Let's take a look at the QQQ and see how a covered call trade might be constructed.

In Fig. 4.1 is a graph of the QQQ showing the 30-day moving average as well as the MACD and Stochastic indicators. Each of these indicators is showing bearish signs as the stock has started to move down.

Whenever a stock I own is showing signs of weakness, I have a decision to make. Should I sell the stock and move on, or perhaps apply the covered call strategy to generate some income that allows me to ride out any expected dip in the price of the stock? Since the purpose of this example is to teach you how to construct a covered call trade, let's assume our goal is to generate some income to ride out the dip. When I personally look at a stock I own to determine my forecast, I always say, *When in doubt, sell the call.*

Figure 4.1 Signal Chart of the NASDAQ-100 (QQQ)

The reason is that when I sell a call I'm guaranteed to generate some income no matter what the stock does. If the stock drops, the income will give me some cushion to absorb the dip. If the stock doesn't move, I will have generated some nice income even though the stock didn't move, and if the stock rises, I know that I will have made a profit, even though it may not have been as much as if I had not done the covered call strategy. I like the odds in all three scenarios so I often sell covered calls on my stocks every single month no matter what my forecast is for the next 30 days.

Let's take a look at the option prices to determine which call to sell and see how much income it will generate.

Fig 4.2 is a quote table for the call option on the QQQ that was roughly 3 weeks from expiration at the time this table was generated.

The strike prices of the call options are listed on the right in bold. The stock is currently trading for $39.30. Think of selecting the price at which you would be willing to sell your stock, should it rise above that price by the expiration day of the option in three weeks. The lower the price you select, the larger the premium (income) you will collect.

Bid Price – The current price a market maker is willing buy your contract or share. It is ultimately the suggested selling price.

I typically select the call option that is closest to the current price of the stock to maximize the income of the strategy. In this case I would select the $40 call option. The income I would collect is based upon the **Bid price** of this option. The bid price of the $40 call is $0.45 or $45 per contract. By selling one of these call options for each 100 shares of QQQ stock I own I can collect $45, which equates to just over 1.1% return for about three weeks.

Calls							Strike Price
Symbol	Last	Chg	Bid	Ask	Vol	Int	
QAV JX	14.60	0.00	14.70	14.90	0	540	24.0
QAV JY	14.12	0.00	13.70	13.90	0	548	25.0
QAV JZ	13.10	0.00	12.70	12.90	0	141	26.0
QAV JA	12.70	0.00	11.70	11.90	0	18	27.0
QAV JB	11.20	0.00	10.70	10.90	0	239	28.0
QAV JC	10.40	0.00	9.70	9.90	0	71	29.0
QAV JD	9.60	0.00	8.70	8.90	0	10,735	30.0
QAV JE	8.90	0.00	7.70	7.90	0	645	31.0
QAV JF	7.80	0.00	6.70	6.90	0	366	32.0
QAV JG	6.50	0.00	5.70	5.90	0	846	33.0
QAV JH	5.60	0.00	4.70	4.90	0	1,968	34.0
QQQ JI	3.90	-0.70	3.80	3.90	154	2,673	35.0
QQQ JJ	2.85	-0.60	2.80	2.90	349	16,528	36.0
QQQ JK	1.90	-0.50	1.85	1.95	934	21,755	37.0
QQQ JL	1.05	-0.40	1.00	1.05	9	57,476	38.0
QQQ JM	0.40	-0.25	0.65	0.70	26	133,300	39.0
QQQ JN	0.10	-0.05	0.45	0.50	12	221,522	40.0
QQQ JO	0.05	0.00	0.00	0.05	50	60,127	41.0

Figure 4.2 Option Chain of the NASDAQ-100 (QQQ) with the $40 Strike price highlighted.

If the stock is above $40 on the third Friday in October when this option expires, my stock will be called away at $40 and I will keep the $0.45 that I collected from the covered call, making my net selling price $40.45. I would only do this trade if I would be happy selling my stock for $40.45 in the next three weeks, since that is the maximum potential profit of this specific trade and would equate to slightly over 2.9%.

Ask Price – The current price a market maker is willing to sell a contract or share. It is ultimately the suggested buying price.

If the stock is anywhere below $40 on the third Friday in October, I would keep my stock and the $45 per contract I collected from the covered calls. This would provide me with $0.45 per share of downside protection against a dip in the QQQ.

Using the QQQ for covered calls is a great way to create a simple cash flow investing business. The QQQ is an easy security to follow because of its tremendous volume and fairly priced options. Due to the diversity offered by the QQQ, it's a great vehicle for getting started in investing and learning the covered call strategy.

Once you master the basics of the covered call strategy there are several more advanced approaches that you might choose to employ to potentially increase your income and growth potential. Start by evaluating the QQQ each 30-day period coinciding with the options expiration cycle to determine the forecast. When bullish, leave the stock uncovered and enjoy the benefit of growth when the stock rises in value. At any time during the month if you see weakness in the stock you would immediately initiate a covered call play to hedge your stock position and generate some income.

By timing my covered call plays on the QQQ to coincide with weakness in the stock I can enjoy the benefit of growth when the stock is rising and income when it's flat or declining. This small adjustment to the timing of your covered call plays can result in a dramatic increase in your overall profit. I like to call this twist on the covered call strategy the *growth vs. income* approach to covered calls.

Here are a few simple steps to help you get started generating income from your portfolio using the covered call strategy.

1. Open an option account
2. Begin to purchase shares of QQQ
3. Check current month call options to sell
4. Sell call options and collect a cash flow/paycheck
5. Manage your position until expiration
6. Repeat Steps 1-5 during the next month

1. **Open an option account** – This requires some additional paperwork at your brokerage firm. Option trading can be very conservative or very risky so the brokerage firm will assign you a level of permission to trade options. There are typically 5 levels of option trading at most firms. All you need to trade covered calls is level 1. If you have a couple thousand dollars in your account and you have traded stocks in the past, you'll likely be approved for level 1. The covered call strategy is actually more conservative than owning stock outright since you collect some income that provides a cushion on the downside

2. **Buy some shares of the QQQ to start building your portfolio** – When you buy one share of the QQQ you're basically getting an interest in all 100 companies that make up the Nasdaq 100. It's like a one stock diversified portfolio, which is not only a good reason to trade it, but the diversification allows you to reduce risk. The risk is reduced in the same manner as if you were to purchase a variety of stocks from different economic sectors, such as retail, technology, oil, medical device, gaming, etc., to minimize the impact of a specific area of the

marketplace, such as only retail companies, when only buying stock in one company.

3. **Check out the call option prices for the QQQ for the current month to see what income you can generate from the covered call strategy** – At most brokerage firms you can bring up the option quotes for any stock by simply clicking on the *option chain* or *option quote* link on the stock quote page. The options will normally be listed in order by strike price. Remember the closer the strike price to the current price of the stock, the higher the premium, and thus the higher the income from the covered call play. When in doubt, I like to pick the strike price that is closest to the current price of the stock to maximize the income potential

4. **Sell your call options and collect your monthly paycheck** – You can sell one call option for each 100 shares of optionable stock you own. There is no requirement to cover all your shares unless you choose to. Selling a call option without owning at least 100 shares of the stock is called a **naked call** and as the name implies, it's one of the riskiest option strategies you can do because if your option is executed and you are required to deliver a stock you do not own, you will be forced to purchase the stock at the current price. The current price may be at a value your account does not have the cash to purchase and will result in a large financial debt. If you're only approved

> Naked Call Option – Similar to a Short Sale of a Stock, a Naked Call Option is selling a call contract without having the shares to meet the obligation of the contract when called away.

for level 1 trading, your broker will not allow you to place a naked option trade, which requires at least a marginable account.

5. **Manage your position and take follow-up action** – Once you enter a covered call trade the only thing you really need to watch is the price of the stock to know where you are. If the stock is higher than your strike price on expiration day (the third Friday of the designated month) you'll be automatically called away from your stock without having to do anything. The transaction is implied in the original covered call trade order. If the price is lower, you'll get to keep the stock and be free to sell another covered call for the next month out and collect another paycheck from your portfolio. Get out of the stock if your stock goes too far south – even in a covered call play you're still at risk of losing money if the stock drops more than the income you collect from the covered call. So you have to be prepared to get out of your stock if things get really bad. Really bad can be a simple calculation of the stock purchase price minus the collected premiums and then subtract an additional 10% stop loss amount.

   When you're in a covered call play you can't just sell your stock without first closing out the covered calls. That would create a naked call play. So if you want to close out a covered call play to stop losing money on your stock position, you must first buy back the covered call you sold. Simply place an order for the exact same call option that you sold to enter your trade in the same quantity. You'll be buying these calls at the asking price. This will offset your covered calls and leave your stock uncovered. Now simply sell the stock and exit the position.

6. **Repeat the process** – the power of this strategy is in the repetition from month to month. This approach to investing is designed to provide a source of consistent monthly income from your investments while still allowing you to participate in the growth of the market.

Every investor should learn how to sell covered calls so they can have one more tool to help them make money when stocks are not in a strong Bullish trend. Anyone can make money when stocks are rising, but few know how to keep the cash coming in when stocks go flat or start falling. The covered call strategy is generally viewed as profit limiting strategy based on the maximum being the premium plus the difference between the purchase price and the locked in selling price (Strike Price). However, the covered call strategy, when properly applied, is one of the few investment strategies that actually make it possible for an investor to profit in rising, falling or flat markets, which is certainly better than making nothing at all during less opportune market conditions.

Chapter 5

Dividends from Value Stocks with the Covered Call Strategy

We have established that the covered call strategy is one used throughout the trading community for the simple fact that it is easy to use and allows the seller of the contracts control of the risk. Also, as stated in the previous chapter, to trade using the covered call strategy the trader starts by first buying and owning shares in lots of 100 shares. The first draw-back to trading covered calls from the nay-sayers is perhaps the excessive amounts of capital tied up in the trade. The amount of capital is obvious; but consider just how much or little risk is truly involved in this strategy.

To determine the risk in the amount of capital let's take a more intimate look into the actual trade. First, the type of stock is one that is generally considered a low risk stock for three main reasons.

1. Large Capitalization Company.
2. 1,000,000 shares or more of average daily volume.
3. Dividend Yield between 1-3% annually.

Of course, if the company pays a relatively high dividend, the trade can be that much more profitable. However, the likelihood of a solid value company isn't just stable with low volatility but is optionable and pays large dividends is easier said than done. The long-term outlook is to see growth in the value company based on consistent earnings, which will enable the company to pay consistent and reliable dividends. Now that we have our stable dividend-paying stock that is traded on a regular basis, which increases our liquidity, we could expect the open interest in the option market to have a relatively similar interest level as found in the stock volume.

Ask yourself, *If all that was traded was the stock itself, could it make a profit?* If the answer is no, stop right there because if it is not worth owning as a standalone stock purchase then it is not a good stock for this strategy. The covered call portion of the strategy is an add-on used to make a good stock trade great.

The dividend, a quarterly payment paid per share by the company represented by the stock, is the first source of profit in the trade. The addition of the dividend payment is what draws many to the stock in the first place. A stock that has a track record of a price increase of 1-3% annually is very nice to have in many portfolios. However, 1-3% is certainly not the sexiest number ever heard of while investing in the stock market. This is especially true when the market has historically increased approximately 6% annually. Remember, the ideal stock also pays a 1-3% dividend annually. This together totals 2-6% annually and is a bit easier to have and hold in a portfolio while maintaining a relatively low risk position. Still nothing to beat a broker up over yet but does give heartburn to the local savings bank account.

Let us not forget this strategy is meant to be a low risk way to generate or increase productivity of owning longer term value stocks. Assume for a moment we have Proctor & Gamble (PG) in our portfolio, the current price being $55.78 and assume that one year ago it was $53.66. This annual increase equates to $2.12 or 3.95%. The volume is well over a million shares a day and if you have any question of the longevity and success of a company such as Proctor & Gamble just open the door to any home in America and observe the long list of products found that are produced by P&G. This is one of the characteristics of a value company. As large as a company like Proctor & Gamble may be, their ability to enter into new economic markets and grow their company becomes difficult due to the fact that there is no place to explore. They are already all over the globe, and makes it difficult to increase revenue and/or earnings. The idea of buying Proctor & Gamble and trading it for quick profits is an entirely different strategy; however, the stock as a value company does fit nicely into this strategy so far.

The next requirement is based on the dividends. P&G currently, at the time of compiling this information, pays an annual dividend of 2%. The 2% falls directly in the center of our target range of 1-3%. The final step that brings this strategy all together is the covered call option trade.

Before moving onto the final step, we must first complete the discussion of the risk associated with our stock position. The stock, Proctor & Gamble in the example, is first purchased for the perceived value in owning the stock for shareholder price increases. For whatever other reasons why the stock happens to be within your personal portfolio, the large, liquid, and stable growth patterned stock has been purchased. The risk is low due the lack of volatile price fluctuations, more than sufficient liquidity and the sheer size and market share of the company. To analyze the stability even further, consider looking into the time frame the company has been paying the current dividend rate or paying dividends at all.

A stock that has recently begun to pay dividends and has made plenty of noise in the growth stock scene is none other than Microsoft. Microsoft is a great stock in the eyes of many traders and investors alike. There are many stories, articles or publications making reference to the success that the Microsoft stock has had in the recent past. Though this is true, this does not make it a viable candidate for this particular strategy, at least not yet. Microsoft, unlike Proctor & Gamble, has only been paying dividends for a relatively short period of time. Therefore with a short track record of paying dividends, the risk in buying Microsoft solely for the dividend increases. In addition, the price fluctuations are significantly greater over shorter periods of time than for companies like Proctor and Gamble, again making it difficult to trade within this particular strategy with its increasing risk.

Even though the dividends are paid at the discretion of the company and do change over time, in both positive and negative directions, consistency is an easy way to evaluate risk. The longer the time frame dividends have been paid with little to no variation in the dividend yield amount, the lower the risk for the particular strategy.

Make note that reward is directly tied to risk. Ask any entrepreneur and a greater percent of them would agree that their big pay day came from assuming a large amount of risk. Or better yet ask the spouse of this entrepreneur to find out how stressful the risk was and then how rewarding it was when it all worked out.

The bigger the risk, generally the larger the reward potential.

The Dividend Paying Stock Covered Call trading strategy is not meant to reduce risk and increase reward. Rather, it is to *control* risk and maintain *consistent* results for the diversification of a portfolio of any size where not all the capital can be used for active and/or aggressive trading strategies.

The ideal situation when identifying the value of the company from the standpoint of purchasing the stock for the perceived value of the dividend is in the long term consistency of paying the dividend yield. The yield is important because the stock can pay the exact same dividend amount annually with a drop in stock price, which will result in an increase of the dividend yield. By recognizing the consistency in the yield percent shows that as the price changes over time, so does the dividend payout amount per share. To illustrate this point consider the following example of the stock price movement with an unchanged dividend payout amount of $1.

Stock Symbol: XYZ

	1998	1999	2000	2001
Price	$20	$21	$22	$23
Div	$1	$1	$1	$1
Yield	5%	4.7%	4.5%	4.3%

Figure 5.1 Decreasing dividend yield as price increases

Dividend yield is tied directly to the price of the stock. As discussed earlier, if the price has little fluctuation over a year and the yield percent remains consistent then the only other way to make money on this stock is to rent it or sell covered calls. A potential increase to risk, sometimes a negative to long-term ownership of this stock, and often times easily overlooked, is a sudden fluctuation in the dividend yield that offers a false sense of value. A perfect example of this is the stock that is located through a search looking for stocks paying high dividend yield. Sometimes this can be due to the response rate of the company to the extreme speed of the market price fluctuations.

Consider for a moment a stock that is priced at $50 and pays an annual dividend of $2.50 or 5%. An earnings announcement is released that is not received well by the market institutions and the price drops from $50 to $25. The drop is immediately reflected in the dividend yield which increases to 10%.

Many traders and investors prefer a stock that pays a 10% dividend yield but dislike the instability of a stock that drops 50% on bad earnings. The process of evaluating the value of a value stock will be determined in the longevity of the dividend yield that changes as the price of the stock changes. The ideal situation is, as the stock price increases 1-3% a year, the dividend payout increases at a relatively equal rate. From the standpoint of a long-term value stock investor, you would generally prefer the stock price to increase over time and the dividend to increase as the company makes more money as reflected in the earning announcements.

Stock Symbol: XYZ

	1998	1999	2000	2001
Price	$20	$21	$22	$23
Div	$1.00	$1.05	$1.10	$1.15
Yield	5%	5%	5%	5%

Figure 5.2 Consistent dividend yield as price increases

With the ideal stock in-hand, how does the trade evolve from here? The first thing is that the stock must be optionable (trading on the option market). Our example used a bit earlier, Proctor & Gamble, is optionable therefore proceed to Step 2. Step 2 involves the technical analysis of the stock itself.

Simple Moving Average (SMA) – A smooth line representing the average closing price over the last number of time periods, such as 30 days.

Technical analysis can go in many directions and will vary from trader to trader as to which technical indicators are used for entry or exit signals. An example of a technical indicator is the **Simple Moving Average** which is a staple throughout the technical trading arena used to show the smooth line based on the average closing prices during a pre-determined time period. Another reasonably common technical process is determining the levels of support and resistance. **Support** and **resistance** levels are very important in this particular strategy when determining which option strike price to sell because it identifies price points where the stock is most likely to slow, stop, or reverse price direction. Adding the premium to the bottom line of an account balance can increase the return of the stock owned from 2-6% annually to 4-12% annually through proper placement of covered calls.

Support – Horizontal price level where the stock price tends to stop decreasing and hold or reverse. The Bottom.

Resistance – Horizontal price level where the stock price tends to stop increasing and hold or reverse. The Top.

Out-the-money (OTM) – An option contract strike price that currently has no intrinsic value.

In-the-money (ITM) – An option contract strike price that currently has intrinsic value.

At-the-money (ATM) – An option contract strike price that is closest to the current underlying stock's price.

Looking at a current price of Proctor & Gamble and considering the stability of the stock price, it is less likely the premium for an **out-the-money** contract will be of much value on the current month contract. This is generally true because most traders are aware of the same things you are looking at…a strong, stable company that is not expected to have a sudden jump in the stock price. This being the case, the current contract will not have enough time for the stock price to move above the out-the-money strike price and very few are willing to pay to speculate to that fact. Therefore, first determine where the resistance level is located. Then attempt to sell the contract strike price that is above the resistance level. This alone will greatly reduce the chance of being called away from the stock and if the stock were to experience a price break out the trade would still be able to capture some of the breakout.

Because we are trying to sell a contract out of the normal price movement range there are less speculating traders that want to buy the contracts, which in turn causes the selling price to be less than the previous month. To make this strategy worthwhile, consider selling contracts with more time value, such as 2 to 3 months of time until expiration. The more time the speculating trader has to allow the underlying stock price to increase, the better chance they will pay a higher premium for the chance to be right on their speculation of price movement.

To better illustrate this process, view the following screen shots of a stock and option chain of a typical value stock.

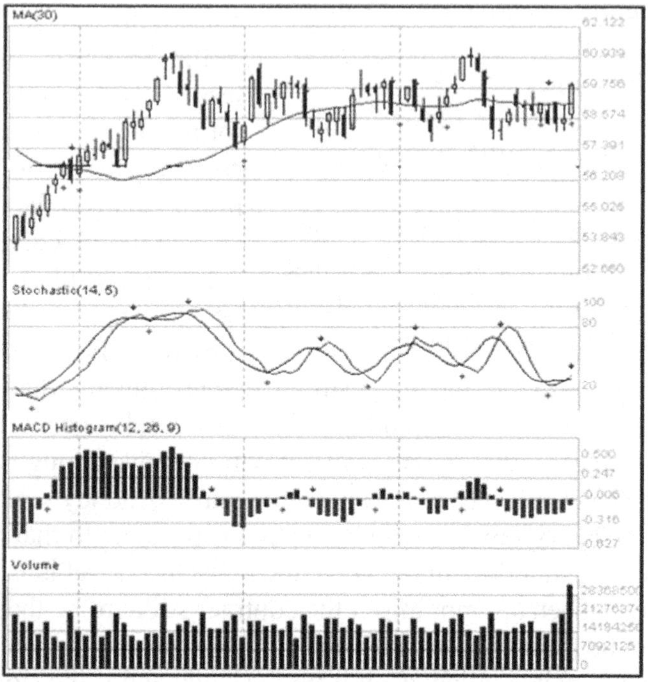

Figure 5.3 Signal Chart of Exxon Mobil (XOM)

The stock, XOM, Exxon Mobil Corp. is certainly large enough and as illustrated in Fig.5.3 is experiencing price channeling for the last 2 ½ months between an easily identified support and resistance. The support level is approximately $57.50 and the resistance level is approximately $60.50. At the time of this evaluation the annual dividend was $1.16 (1.97% dividend yield). Next, the option chain must be evaluated. The evaluation is to decide which strike price optimizes the maximum return and minimizes the trade risk. To reduce risk due to the time of market exposure, attempt to sell contracts with less time, but at the same time sell out-the-money contracts to increase the potential of maintaining ownership of the stock at the end of the contract month.

Calls						Strike Price
Last	Chg	Bid	Ask	Vol	Int	
36.60	0.00	34.10	34.30	0	932	22.5
29.90	0.00	31.60	31.80	0	431	25.0
25.40	0.00	26.60	26.70	0	872	30.0
20.40	0.00	21.60	21.80	0	6,227	35.0
16.00	0.00	16.70	16.90	0	13,326	40.0
11.90	0.50	11.90	12.10	74	17,081	45.0
7.40	0.70	7.50	7.70	1	14,910	50.0
3.91	0.61	3.90	4.10	737	29,294	55.0
1.65	0.20	1.60	1.65	3	57,571	60.0
0.60	0.00	0.55	0.65	1	82,284	65.0
0.22	-0.03	0.20	0.25	118	35,221	70.0
0.10	0.00	0.10	0.15	4	36,438	75.0
0.05	0.00	0.05	0.10	0	12,689	80.0
0.05	0.00	0.00	0.05	0	157	85.0

Figure 5.4 Option Chain 2 months until expiration (XOM)

Exxon Mobil is showing the increased expectations in the premiums. (Perhaps this is due to the increased publicity of oil and gasoline.) For a contract that is out 2 months, the premium is paying $1.60 per share for the first out-the-money contract. The stock price is currently $59.24 making the $60 strike and the $65 strike prices both out-the-money contracts. Which option contract strike price should be sold within the parameters of this strategy?

Because the approximate resistance level is $60.50, the $60 strike price is more likely to be called away within the expected range of the stock price. Another way to view this strike price is by asking what extra value does the strategy offer to sell at $60 if the stock price goes up to $60.50. The premium, which is $1.60, added to the strike price is the same as selling the stock at $61.60. The selling price remains beneficial with a profit of $1.10. If you wanted to repeat the process and make sure you are on the books as a share holder in time for the next dividend payment, consider buying the stock shortly after being called away or buying back the contract before it expires. Just note, buying the contract back is possible but is generally done at a loss to the trade due to the increased amount of cost associated with the option contract, but is done to remain in control of the stock and be able to apply the covered call strategy next month.

If possible, consider the strike price that is above the resistance level. In this example, the strike price would be the $65 strike. Selling the $65 strike price reduces the expected sale of the stock at the end of the contract month based on the resistance level. In this case the premium of $0.55 is quite a bit less than the $60 strike but the addition of the premium to the bottom line is something many have given up by not knowing about the trade at all. This is money being left on the table each quarter on a stock that was considered a longer term position. Do not settle for the increase of the stock value alone; add the covered call contract along with dividends to make a solid value company a cash flow tool in any portfolio.

The actual numbers for this example would look like this:

Stock purchase price	= $59.24
Annual 1.5% growth	= $0.89
Annual Dividend	= $1.16
4 Quarterly CC premiums	=$2.20 ($0.55 x 4)
Total annual increase	= $4.25
Strategy % increase	= 7.17%

Figure 5.5 Example of a Covered Call-Dividend Value Stock Strategy Annual results.

A 7.17% increase on a stock that is not expected to increase more than 1.5% annually is a noticeable difference to any account. The strategy in its basic form is the owning of 100 share lots of a value stock that pays a dividend with a yield between 1-3%. The stock must be optionable. The trader or investor using this approach will make approximately 5 trades a year (a covered call contract sell order once every three months and the initial trade to purchase the stock.)

Always follow your personal trading rules when buying a stock and setting the exit point on a stock that does not respond as projected. An example of an exit strategy is using stop loss orders of a pre-designated percent of the purchase price minus the premium received. However, as discussed earlier, a more detailed and current stop loss price point will be determined and re-evaluated as the underlying stock price changes and the premium is collected, off-setting the actual purchase price.

Chapter 6

Dump Mutual Funds and Beat the Pros at the Trading Game

If you've ever invested a penny in an index-based mutual fund, this may be the most important chapter you've ever read. The mutual fund industry's most popular product has just been made obsolete by a simple investment tool called an **Exchange Traded Fund (ETF)**.

Exchange Traded Fund (ETF) – A security that trades like a stock and experiences price changes throughout the trading day as a result of buying and selling. The ETF tracks the movement of a corresponding index, commodity, or group of diversified securities.

Since the launch of the first ETF in 1993, over $170 Billion has been invested into over 150 different ETFs. These new investments offer so many advantages over index mutual funds that investors are shifting billions of dollars into them even as we speak.

Now more than ever, investors have a viable alternative to investing their money in a mutual fund or trying to create their own diversified portfolio of individual stocks. Given the 2003 mutual fund scandals as an example, (where the mutual fund companies were accused of market timing and over charging fees and later had to pay over $500 million to the SEC and $160 million in fee reductions as part of the settlement) is now a good time to reconsider mutual funds and instead learn how ETFs can help accomplish financial objectives and reduce risk?

Worldwide investors are liquidating their shares in mutual funds from industry leaders like the Fidelity Magellan, 20th Century Ultra, Vanguard Index 500 and thousands of other index-based funds to gain the significant advantages offered by ETFs. Here are just a few to consider…

- No more hefty commissions and management fees. ETFs trade like stocks, so you can trade them for less than $10 at many online brokerage firms. Since the ETFs don't change their holdings as frequently as most mutual funds, the management fees are a fraction of the typical fees charged by a traditional mutual fund.

- The performance of an ETF more closely matches the performance of the corresponding index. ETFs follow the indexes much more closely than most index mutual funds.

- Investors can trade in or out of an ETF whenever they want. You can trade an ETF anytime the stock market is open. You don't have to wait until the next day to get out when the market is falling like you do with almost every mutual fund due to various trade rules and restrictions.

- You can use ETFs to generate monthly cash flow from your portfolio. Since some ETFs have options, you can generate consistent monthly income from your investment in an ETF even if it is not moving up.

- ETFs are easy to follow. Buy and sell prices are available anywhere you can get stock quotes, including the Internet and your local newspaper's financial section.

- Simplified Research. Since you're investing in a basket of stocks, there is no cumbersome fundamental research to do on individual company financials and reports.

- ETFs are a perfect vehicle for investors who want to apply market timing strategies using the latest investment tracking tools. You can apply some of the most powerful new investment tools online to move in and out of the ETF to enhance performance and minimize risk.

- ETFs are a simple one investment portfolio. Just one share of an ETF offers the same diversification as the index it's based on. Buy one share of the SPY and have the same diversity as owning each stock in the S&P 500.

- ETFs still earn dividends. Even though you don't actually own the stocks in the Index, you have the opportunity to earn quarterly dividends on them. Since more and more stocks are beginning to pay dividends and the taxes you pay on dividends have just been dramatically reduced, ETFs make even more sense.

- Save money on capital gains taxes. These investments are very tax efficient compared to mutual funds and can minimize your exposure to taxes on your gains. You control when you sell, so you also control when you incur a tax consequence from your investment. With mutual funds, your tax consequences are determined by the fund manager and you have no control.

- You can even place stop orders to get you out when the index makes a sudden correction. In a volatile market like we have today, this is one more reason an investment in an ETF gives you more control and more peace of mind.

- Invest with leverage. Since these are stocks, you can buy them on **margin** to add leverage to your investment.

Margin – A line of credit extended in specially designated brokerage accounts requiring an additional application process.

- IRA approved. You can invest your entire retirement account in tracking stocks to create a simple, well-diversified portfolio of the best performing stocks.

- Short selling is OK. Now if you feel the market is going down, you can short-sell the entire index to profit from the decline. Best of all, you can even do this on a downtick, something that's not allowed on most stocks.

Sound too good to be true? It's not. Let's look at these ETFs a bit closer to help you understand exactly how to use them to maximize your investment in the stock market, simplify your investing and secure your financial future.

What is an ETF?

ETFs are an investment product created by the American Stock Exchange. In this report we are going to focus on three of the most popular indexes and their respective ETFs, the S&P 500 (SPY), the Dow Jones Industrial Average (DIA), and the NASDAQ 100 (QQQ).

Each of these indexes has a **tracking stock** on the American Stock Exchange that investors can purchase just as they would any other stock. These stocks are designed to mirror the movement and dividend yield of the stocks that make up each of these indexes. When the index moves up, so does the tracking stock. It's a simple way for the average investor to closely duplicate the

> Tracking Stock – A common stock issued by a parent company that tracks the price movement of the company or index with no claim to the assets of the parent company. The most popular is the QQQ for the Nasdaq 100 Index.

performance of the most widely followed baskets of stocks in the world.

Underlying each of the tracking stocks is a trust, created by the American Stock Exchange and funded by wealthy investors and institutions. These unit investment trusts actually purchase and own shares in the companies that make up the index. The trusts are designed so that the performance of the tracking stock will closely mirror the actual movement of the index itself. The trusts are also established with a long-term time frame in mind which gives it the risk expectancy of a value stock, discussed earlier. The trusts are designed to exist into the 22nd century at a minimum. Since the trusts incur lower management fees and lower tax consequences than most index mutual funds, their performance is typically much closer to the actual performance of the index itself. This is one of the major advantages of tracking the stock over an index mutual fund.

You can purchase shares of the tracking stocks from any broker just as you would any individual company stock. There is no minimum investment, like the stipulations many mutual funds have, so this is a very affordable way for any investor to get started in investing. You can buy one share or thousands of shares just as easy. Even with an account as small as $1000 you can get the same diversity as much larger investors.

Since each of these indexes are made up of different stocks, let's look at the specifics of each of the three most popular ETF s, the SPY, DIA, and the QQQ.

The S&P 500 (symbol – SPY, also called the Spider)

The ticker symbol SPY tracks the S&P 500 and is more commonly referred to as the *Spider*. This symbol and nickname was derived from the ETF being based on Standard and Poor's Depositary Receipts (SPDRs) Index. Standard and Poor's maintains the index of 500 stocks and the spider tracks the performance of that index. These are high capitalization companies like Microsoft, Dell, Boeing, American Express, Marriott, Wal-Mart and others. These are not the largest stocks or the best stocks, but a list of leading stocks in leading industries that form the foundation of the US stock market. Since this index is made up of 500 stocks, it has the highest degree of diversification of the three tracking stocks being considered in this report based on the largest pool of stocks.

The spider represents 1/10th of the actual value of the S&P 500 index. In other words, when the index is trading at 1200, the spider will be priced at $120 per share.

Fig 6.1 and Fig 6.2 are examples of the S&P 500 Index and the SPY taken at the same time

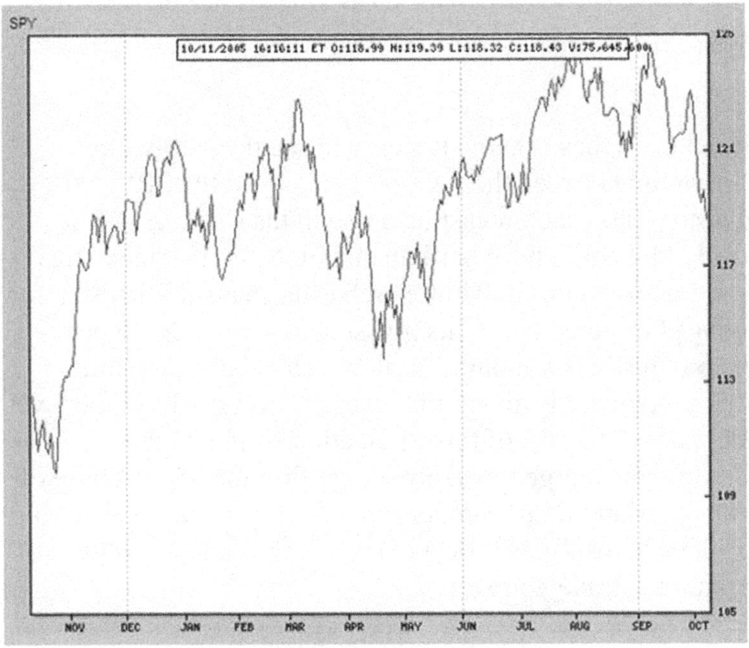

Figure 6.1 Trend Chart of the S&P 500 (SPY).

Figure 6.2 Trend Chart of the S&P 500 Index (SPX).

Based upon these charts, it's easy to see the nearly direct correlation between the S&P 500 index and the SPY. An investor who was forecasting a rise in the stock market in April 2004 could have participated in the bullish move that lasted until August 2004 by purchasing shares of the SPY for about $115 per share. This investment grew to $125 per share in just a few months producing a handsome return. This investment is diversified over the 500 stocks in the S&P 500 index. The cost of this transaction would be the commission charged by a brokerage firm for the purchase of a stock. Many online brokers are offering stock trades for up to 5000 shares for as little as $10, which is a low cost way of placing the trade yourself.

The shares in the SPY can be sold anytime the market is open. If the investor were to change from a bullish forecast to a bearish one, they could simply enter an order to sell any or all of their shares through their broker and get out of the market. No waiting till the end of the day or the next day to discover at what price you sold, like it is with mutual funds.

Any time the market is open for trading the SPY will have a BID and ASK price listed. The Ask price is the price you would be charged at that time to purchase shares, and the Bid price would be the price you would get if you were selling shares at that time. The bid and ask price change constantly through the day as the S&P 500 index changes. If the S&P 500 index were to rise 20 points during a day, that would theoretically translate into a $2 rise in the price of the SPY.

The profit earned from investing in the SPY is calculated the same way you would calculate the profit on any stock transaction. You simply subtract the cost for your shares (including commissions) from the selling price of your shares (less commissions). The difference is your profit. It's simple, fast, and efficient.

Dow Jones Industrial Average (symbol – DIA, also called the Diamonds)

The DIA, or Diamonds, track the Dow Jones Industrial Average. This index is probably the most widely followed index of the US stock market. This tracking stock represents the first time in the over 100 year history of the Dow Jones Industrial Average, that the Dow Jones Company has licensed their name for a financial product. The license was given to the American Stock Exchange, the exchange where the Diamonds are traded, hence its name.

The Dow is made up of 30 large companies considered to best represent the cross section of the U.S. economy. Fig 6.3

shows the current list of companies in the Dow with their weighting in the average and their price at the time this table was created.

Company	Ticker	Wghtg.	US$ Close
3M Co.	MMM	8130	81.3
Alcoa Inc.	AA	3252	32.52
Altria Group Inc.	MO	4898	48.98
American Express Co.	AXP	4963	49.63
American International Group Inc.	AIG	7088	70.88
Boeing Co.	BA	5187	51.87
Caterpillar Inc.	CAT	7225	72.25
Citigroup Inc.	C	4641	46.41
Coca-Cola Co.	KO	4435	44.35
E.I. DuPont de Nemours & Co.	DD	4224	42.24
Exxon Mobil Corp.	XOM	4513	45.13
General Electric Co.	GE	3257	32.57
General Motors Corp.	GM	4110	41.1
Hewlett-Packard Co.	HPQ	1792	17.92
Home Depot Inc.	HD	3653	36.53
Honeywell International Inc.	HON	3568	35.68
Intel Corp.	INTC	2159	21.59
International Business Machines Corp.	IBM	8440	84.4
Johnson & Johnson	JNJ	5754	57.54
JPMorgan Chase & Co.	JPM	3910	39.1
McDonald's Corp.	MCD	2700	27
Merck & Co. Inc.	MRK	4493	44.93
Microsoft Corp.	MSFT	2728	27.28
Pfizer Inc.	PFE	3229	32.29
Procter & Gamble Co.	PG	5551	55.51
SBC Communications Inc.	SBC	2580	25.8
United Technologies Corp.	UTX	9331	93.31
Verizon Communications Inc.	VZ	3903	39.03
Wal-Mart Stores Inc.	WMT	5320	53.2
Walt Disney Co.	DIS	2240	22.4

Figure 6.3 List of 30 stocks that together equate to the Dow Jones 30.

The Diamonds represent 1/100th of the value of the Dow. In other words, if the Dow was at 10,500, then the DIA would be trading for \$105 per share. When the Dow rises by 100 points, the DIA would rise by \$1 per share. Just like the SPY, the performance of the DIA is tied to the performance of the Dow.

Following is a chart of the Dow followed by another chart showing the DIA. These charts were captured at the same time.

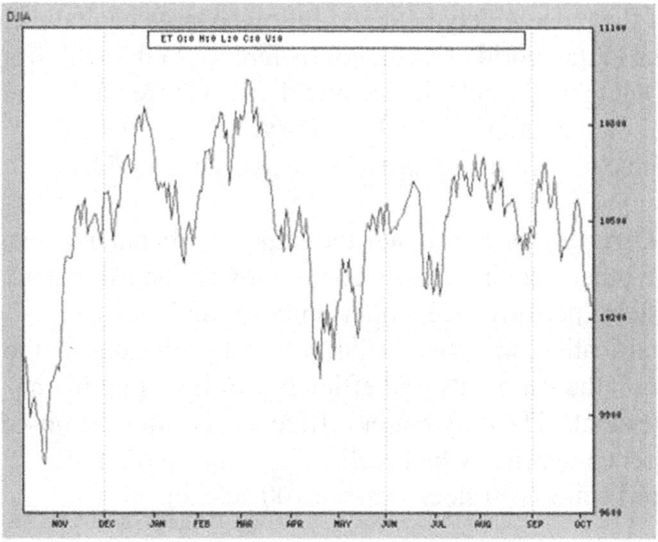

Figure 6.4 Trend Chart of the Dow Jones Industrial Average (DJIA).

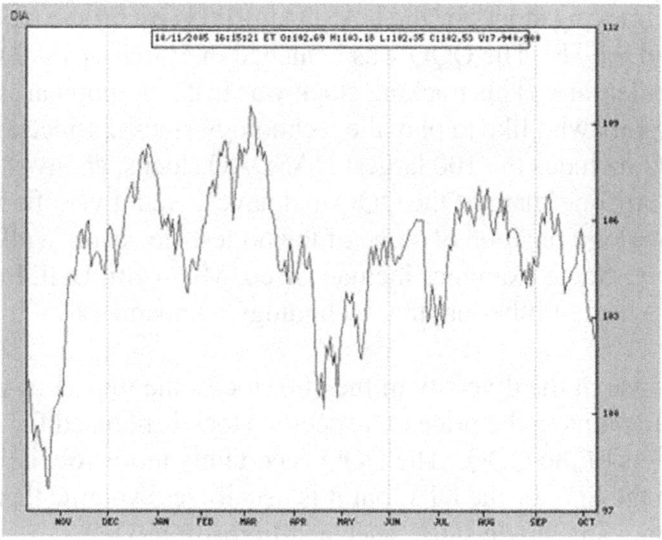

Figure 6.5 Trend Chart of the Dow Jones 30 (DIA).

Investors who wish to have a portfolio of *blue chip* stocks can invest in the DIA and have a well diversified portfolio of

30 of the most widely held and followed large capitalization stocks in the world. One major difference in the DIA from the QQQ and the SPY is that any dividends are paid monthly rather than quarterly, which means you do not need to continue to own the security to receive some dividends.

The DIA affords an investor the same significant advantages of the other tracking stocks, such as lower commissions, long-term performance, opportunity for dividends, diversification, margin capabilities, and short sales, not to mention the simplicity and efficiency of investing in one single stock. The only major difference, besides the obvious difference in price, which will vary, is the amount of diversification (30 stocks versus 100 stocks).

NASDAQ 100 (symbol – QQQ, also called the Q's)

The tracking stock for the NASDAQ 100 is by far the most popular ETF. The QQQ was launched in March of 1999 to great fanfare. This tracking stock was instantly popular with investors who like to play the technology stocks. Since the QQQ includes the 100 largest NASDAQ stocks, an investor can buy one share of the QQQ and have a well diversified technology position of some of the hottest stocks on Wall Street. Some examples include Cisco, Microsoft, Dell, Intel and a host of other popular technology companies.

Because of the diversity of the 100 stocks, the impact of wild fluctuations in the price of a specific stock is reduced for holders of the QQQ. The QQQ is certainly more volatile than the SPY or the DIA, but it is usually less volatile than owning any single stock, such as Microsoft or Dell.

The QQQ is priced at approximately $1/20^{th}$ of the actual NASDAQ 100. In other words, if the NASDAQ 100 is trading at 2400, then the QQQ will be approximately $120 per share. When the NASDAQ 100 rises by 20 points, the QQQ should increase approximately $1.

Fig. 6.6 and Fig. 6.7 are charts of the Nasdaq-100 index and the QQQ from about the same time.

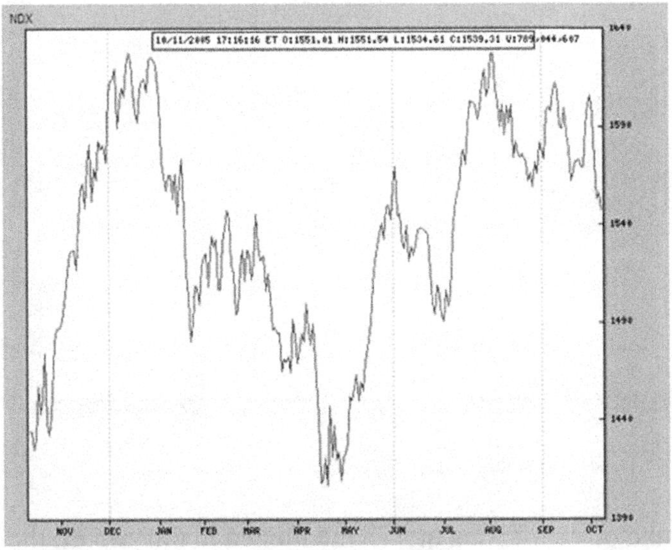

Figure 6.6 Trend Chart of the Nasdaq-100 Index (NDX).

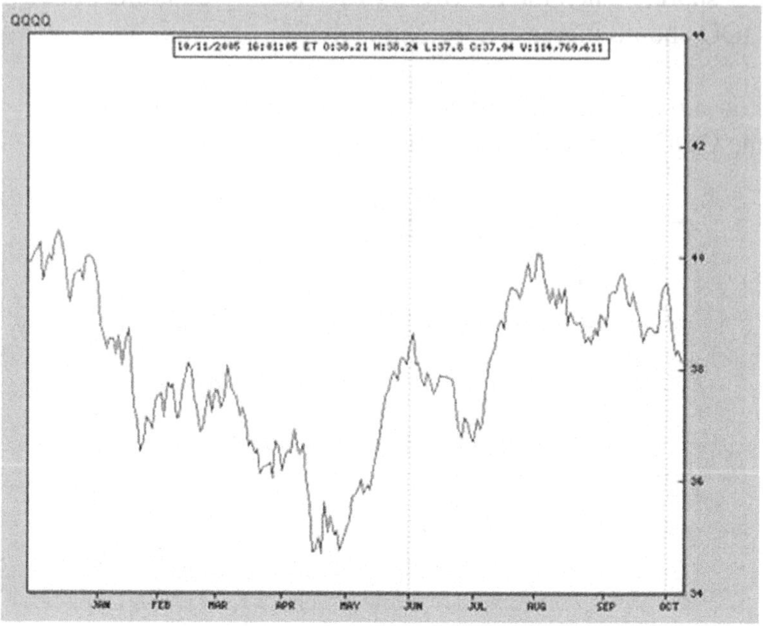

Figure 6.7 Trend Chart of the Nasdaq-100 (QQQ).

Like the other tracking stocks mentioned in this report, the QQQ trades on the NASDAQ Stock Exchange. The stock price fluctuates with the NASDAQ market and current quotes are readily available online or from any brokerage firm. There is no minimum purchase requirement so this investment is available to nearly any investor.

Now that you have a little better idea of what a tracking stock is and how it works, let's review in more detail the specific advantages these new investments offer investors over traditional index mutual funds.

Lower Commissions and Fees

I have always gotten a kick out of hearing investors say they don't pay commissions because they invest in *No Load* mutual funds. How naïve! I've yet to meet a person who works in the financial industry that did it for free. But this is a common misconception by a great number of unsophisticated investors who invest primarily in no load funds.

The real truth is that they are not free and in some cases they are actually very expensive. In fact many of the leading names in the mutual fund industry have been found guilty of price gouging and unfair practices that cost investors hundreds of millions of dollars in fees. Whenever I see the words *No Load,* I know that the fees and commissions are not very obvious and may be difficult to calculate. Unlike when you buy a stock, the fees and commissions on a mutual fund do not appear on your statements, but rather they are deducted from the value of the fund before they determine its actual value. In fact, many no load funds actually charge investors 1-2% per year in fees and expenses that most investors don't even realize they are paying. Now you can see why most index mutual funds can't even beat the averages of indexes they are based on. The fees and expenses they charge to the fund reduce their overall performance and the return to their investors.

In contrast, when you invest in a stock, the commissions are itemized on your trade confirmation slip for you to clearly see. With online brokerage commissions below $10 per trade, the cost savings from investing in tracking stocks could be substantial for many investors.

Another thing to consider is that the management fees for a fund are annual fees that the managers deduct from the fund each year. When you buy a stock, the commission is only charged when you buy and then again when you sell. No commissions are charged to just hold the stock in your account, and no commissions are charged if the stock should rise in value.

For example, if you invested $10,000 in an index mutual fund that had fees and expenses equal to 1% per year, you would be paying $100 in fees each year regardless of whether you made any trades during the year. If you invested that same $10,000 in an ETF and made one trade in and one trade out during the year, your fees would be limited to the commission when you bought and the commission when you sold. In an average discount brokerage account the cost will range from $10 to $50. In fact, there are fees for managing the trusts that underlie the tracking stocks, but they are generally less than 1/5th of a percent per year and can usually be covered out of the dividends that are paid on the stock, so it doesn't come out of the actual equity.

Quite simply, the cost savings alone should be reason enough for most investors to shift their index mutual funds over to ETFs.

Tracking stocks more closely mirror the underlying index

The goal of every index mutual fund manager is to beat the index his or her fund is based upon. The fact is that less than 10% of them actually do it. A big part of the reason is due to the commissions and expenses they charge. Another less obvious reason is the complexity of moving large amounts of money in and out of a limited number of stocks they hold.

For a fund manager who has billions of dollars to invest in the stocks that make up the index, it's a tough job to get in and out as quickly as they would like. When a stock is dropped from the S&P 500 and replaced by a new one, every single S&P 500 index mutual fund must now liquidate the shares they held in the old company and purchase shares in the new company. Considering that there are hundreds of such funds that may hold these shares, it is impossible for them to all liquidate their shares at the same time without severely hurting the price of the stock. The reverse is true too; imagine what 1000 fund managers with billions of dollars to invest could do to a single stock if they all tried to buy it at the same time.

What the fund managers end up doing is *easing* in and out of stocks in the index. So they are not getting the same exact performance as the index because they simply can't be as efficient. This is not the case with tracking stocks and is one of the primary reasons that ETFs are able to match the movement of the index so much more closely.

Buy or sell tracking stocks whenever the market is open

There's nothing worse than to be invested and have the market drop like a rock right before your eyes and know that you can't get out, even if you wanted to. That's the situation with most mutual funds. You place your order to get out, but the price for your order is not set until the end of the trading day or even the next day. A lot can happen in a day in these volatile markets and you can't do a thing about it. That is, unless you invest your money in ETFs.

Since these stocks trade just like any other equity, you can buy or sell shares anytime the market is open. (9:30 AM to 4:00 PM Eastern time) You can use all of the different orders that you would use for any stock purchase, like a market or limit order. Many brokers will also allow you to use **Stop Orders**. A Stop Order is an order that you place to get out of the position automatically if it drops to a certain price level. It's like a safety net to get you out when you're not watching the market and it drops to your predetermined exit point.

If you're like most traders, making a decision to get out of an investment when it's going against you is nearly impossible due to the emotional attachment or the fear of being wrong and having written proof of when the trade is executed. This feature alone is another reason most investors could improve their returns by switching to ETFs from mutual funds.

Generate monthly cash flow from your investments in any market

Many of the most popular ETFs now offer options. And as discuss earlier in the Covered Call Option Strategies, you can generate monthly cash flow from your stock holdings even when they are not moving. The income generated can be as much as 3-5% of the value of the holdings, depending on which ETF you own.

Since the QQQ has options, an investor can apply the covered call strategy to the funds invested in the QQQ to generate monthly income. Since most investors tend to be *buy and hold* investors, they don't make money when the investment they own is not moving up in price. Sometimes an investment may sit at the same price for several weeks or even several months. The Covered Call would be a very low risk strategy that would allow you to earn some income from your investments during this time.

Because the QQQ trades like a stock, you can use some of these traditional stock strategies to enhance the potential returns over what a mutual fund could provide. Covered Calls are one of the few option strategies that are allowed by most brokers in an IRA or other retirement account, so nearly any investor can and should do it.

The risk of using this strategy on your tracking stock is that you give up the potential to make any profits above a certain price (the strike price of your covered call), so there is a limited upside. Most investors who use Covered Calls recognize this risk and are willing to forego a large windfall gain in favor of a smaller more probable monthly gain in the form of income, or cash flow, from Covered Calls.

Easy to follow

A **tracking stock** is a very easy investment to stay on top of. Current quotes are offered in hundreds of places on the Internet and through any brokerage firm's website. Just provide the symbol for the tracking stock and you'll be given a bid and ask price for that stock. The **Ask** price is the price you would have to pay to purchase shares at that moment and the **Bid** price is the price you would be paid if you were selling shares at that moment.

The difference between the Bid and the Ask is called the *Spread.* I like to think of this as the money that the brokerages and exchanges keep for making a fair and liquid market for investors to trade. The market makers basically buy shares at the bid from investors who are selling and then turn around and sell them at the ask price to investors who are buying, keeping the difference for themselves.

Simplified Research

Finding an investment that is suited to your objectives and tolerance for risk can be a very time consuming and difficult process. The ETF's holdings are made up of the actual stocks that comprise the different indexes they track, so you never have to identify a new stock to replace an old one. Investment experts do the selection of stocks for the indexes and their decisions are implemented on the indexes and reflected by the ETFs.

Instead of identifying individual stocks to invest in, an ETF investor simply has to forecast the direction of the overall market or an individual sector of the market. There are no PE ratios to look up or complex formulas to use. Simply using basic stock charts and news you can stay on top of your investments.

Using Charts and technical indicators to make better investment decisions

These give you a big advantage. By using the latest internet investment tools and technology, you can apply some simple indicators to a graph of the ETF to aid in your decision making process. The most commonly used indicators for this purpose are the simple moving average, moving average convergence/divergence (MACD), and Stochastic.

Each of these indicators helps to identify the trend of a stock. Used in combination they help investors make better decisions on when to buy and sell. Positive signals from each of these indicators signal a rising trend in the market and an opportunity to profit as the market moves higher. Negative signals indicate a declining trend in the market and alert investors to sell tracking stocks or short sell them.

Figure 6.8 Signal Chart of the Nasdaq-100 (QQQ).

Fig. 6.8 is a graph of the QQQ showing the three basic indicators noted above. Looking at the far right of the graph at the current activity of the QQQ you will see that the price of the stock just broke down through the 30-day moving average. This is an indication of weakness. At the same time the MACD histogram has recently peaked and has started to decline with a red arrow; a bearish signal. The Stochastic indicator is turning lower with a red arrow which also confirms weakness in the QQQ. Using these simple indicators in conjunction with the price graph and news on the market is a great way to track and forecast the direction of the QQQ.

Diversification

Investment experts all agree that investors should have a well-diversified portfolio of investments. It goes back to the old *all your eggs in one basket* principle. By spreading your money over several different types of investments or among a variety of market sectors, you can reduce your exposure to a sudden decline in any one single investment or sector.

Investing in a tracking stock gives an investor total diversification in one single investment. It would be a difficult task for most people to decide which sectors to invest in and how much of their portfolio to put into each one. When you invest in an ETF, that job is done automatically for you.

You simply choose which ETF you want to invest in and as soon as you buy a single share, your money is diversified over the entire group of companies that comprise that index. When you buy a share of the DIA, you're diversified over the 30 stocks in the Dow. When you buy a share of the SPY, you're diversified over the 500 stocks of the S&P 500, and when you buy a share of the QQQ, you're diversified over the 100 stocks in the NASDAQ 100. Diversification was never so fast and easy.

Earn Dividends

Many investors like to own stocks that pay dividends. When you own an ETF you have the opportunity to earn dividends from the stocks that are in the index. Since the stocks in the index are actually owned by the trust that underlies each

ETF, the trust is earning any dividends that are paid by those companies.

If you own shares of a tracking stock that is earning dividends, your share of the dividends are added to your account when they are paid. The actual dividends paid will not equal the full amount earned by the trust as the trust will usually deduct the small management fees and expenses from these dividends and distribute the net amount to the owners of the shares.

The SPY and the QQQ make dividend distributions on a quarterly basis, whereas the DIA distributes dividends monthly. So the total potential profit of owning a tracking stock is not limited to just the appreciation while you hold them, but is enhanced by any dividend distributions that are made as well. An ETF is designed to mirror the *total return* an investor would earn by holding each of the individual stocks in their own accounts.

Save money on Taxes

Investing in a tracking stock is likely to be more tax-efficient than buying actual shares or mutual funds because the tracking stock merely tracks the movement of the index and is not engaged in active trading of the stocks in the index.

An actively traded mutual fund may incur capital gains taxes for a holder of shares in the fund. The more trading that is done, the more likely the investors will be assessed some capital gains at the end of the year. This is not a huge benefit, but I've yet to meet an investor that didn't want to save every penny on taxes that they possibly could. In the first couple years of the bear market that began in March of 2000, investors in mutual funds received 1099's from their fund managers showing tremendous capital gains that had serious tax consequences. This was difficult for many fund investors to handle when they saw that the value of their funds had declined substantially over the same period of time. I'm all for paying my fair share of taxes on what I earn, but who wants to pay taxes on gains they can't even see? This is just one more small way to minimize the impact of taxes on your investment profits.

Investing with leverage

Some investors like to use leverage to maximize their potential returns from their investments. Most mutual funds do not allow margin buying of their shares, although some employ **margin** buying as part of their approach to investing.

> Margin – A line of credit extended in specially designated brokerage accounts requiring an additional application process.

Brokers are actually very willing to lend money to their clients to buy more stocks. They even offer fairly competitive rates for margin borrowing. Most brokers will allow a client to borrow an amount equal to the value of cash and stock in their account. This allows the investor to buy twice as much stock as they actually have money for.

The idea is to control more stock than you have money for to receive more gains when the stocks rise in value. While this is very attractive when the market is moving in your favor, margin is equally dangerous when the market moves against you. You may make money twice as fast as the market goes up, but you'll also lose it twice as fast as it goes down. The cash and/or stock you have in your account serves as the collateral for the loan. If the value of the collateral should drop below a predetermined level (usually around 35%) the broker will give you a *margin call* and ask you to deposit more stock or cash in your account or risk having some of your stock sold to cover the margin call. I like to say a margin call is basically your broker calling to tell you you're in over your head.

Margin is not for everyone, but for those that want to add some leverage to their index investments, it's nice to know that you can use margin on ETFs. Before you can trade on margin, you will need to establish a margin account with your broker. This involves filling out some additional paperwork to describe your current financial position and your investment objectives. It's also important to note that most brokers won't allow margin buying in a retirement account like an IRA. That is not true of all brokers, so check with your individual firm to find out if they allow margin trading in a qualified retirement account.

IRA approved investments

One of the best ways to trade ETFs is in an IRA or other qualified retirement account like a 401k. This is a great benefit because most people like to have their investment accounts invested in a well-diversified portfolio of stocks for the long-term. What better way to do that than with an ETF.

You don't have to do anything special to get this set up. Just ask your 401k or IRA at a brokerage firm whether they offer individual stock trading as an option. You simply buy shares and hold on to them as long as you want. If you decide to get out of the market, you simply sell the shares at the current market price. It's easy and far less expensive than owning most index mutual funds.

All gains and dividends remain in your retirement account and grow tax deferred or even tax-free if you have a new

Roth IRA. It's a great way to build your retirement account with some of the best returning investments for the long haul.

Short Selling is OK

Short selling is a strategy used to make money when stocks decline in value. With the bear market of the early 2000's still fresh on every investor's mind, it's clear to most investors that stocks don't always go up. The biggest challenge most investors face is what to do when stocks are going down. It's difficult to wake up each day and see the value of your retirement nest egg shrinking.

What few investors realize is that there is just as much opportunity to make money when stocks are going down as when they are rising. One key to trading is knowing which strategies to apply and when to apply them. One strategy that has been used for decades to make money in a bearish market is short-selling.

The goal of every investor is to buy low and sell high. **Short selling** is just the reverse. An investor sells first at what they feel is a high price in hopes that the stock will then decline and give them the opportunity to buy it later at a lower price. Just as in the traditional approach to investing, the profit is the difference between the price paid and the price sold for. It's all just done in reverse.

You must have a margin account to sell stocks short and short selling is not allowed in an IRA. The biggest advantage to short selling ETFs over other stocks is that you are allowed to short them when they are trading down (referred to as a *down tick*). With most stocks, you can't place an order to sell short until there is an uptick in the price of the stock. This may make it difficult to short a stock that is falling fast.

The index mutual fund industry is in big trouble. Once investors understand the significant advantages to investing in ETFs over traditional index mutual funds, business is going to dry up in a hurry. As a clear sign that the mutual fund industry recognizes the threat posed by ETFs, Vanguard, the originator of the index mutual fund concept, recently launched their own ETF product called VIPERs to be competitive in this market.

The advantages are huge and there is simply no good reason not to use these great new investment vehicles now that you know about them. Once you invest in an ETF and see how easy and profitable they can be, you'll be glad you switched.

The popularity of ETFs is only going to grow. There are currently over 150 different ETFs available to investors. Plans are underway to create new ETFs for interest rate markets and even the precious metals markets. There are now ETFs on nearly every major world stock market and individual market sector allowing a virtually unlimited array of investments to diversify your holdings.

To learn more about ETFs and how to use them in your investment plans, check the American Stock Exchange website at www.amex.com. This is where most of the ETFs are traded so you'll be able to find a wealth of information on the latest ETFs and trading strategies associated with these popular investment vehicles. Another great site for learning about ETFs is www.etfconnect.com.

Chapter 7

You Make the Call

Trading and investing in the stock markets can be exciting, rewarding, stressful, overwhelming at times and (most importantly) profitable. You can be one of the most educated individuals in the understanding of how the markets work, why they work and the ideas of profiting in the stock markets, but it really comes down to applying what you have learned. If you have not worked with a mentor you should consider this approach to better appreciate the often overlooked elements of trading.

As discussed in the previous chapters, you have been made aware of a handful of valuable trading strategies. The value is two-fold however. First, you obtain the knowledge and second, you apply the processes you have learned. It is now time to put into action the principles discussed earlier.

Paper trading is a process of simulated trading in the markets without using real money. Paper trading is utilized to learn as much as possible before trading with real money and exposing your account to any level of risk. Remember that anytime your capital is no longer in hand, there is some level of risk being assumed. As an extreme example, the money you have placed in a checking or savings account at your local bank is at risk. Thankfully it doesn't happen often and your account is insured by the federal government. But what if the bank is robbed? There goes your money. Another possibility is using your capital in a trading account that is highly leveraged with margin and/or naked positions.

Paper trading should not be allowed to become a crutch, hindering your progress toward placing and possibly profiting from a real trade. The paper trade process should be used for three reasons; back-testing strategies, testing new strategies in the current market and to build confidence in your ability to correctly recognize when and why to enter or exit a trade.

Purposes of Paper Trading

1. Back-Testing Strategies
2. Test New Strategies
3. Build Confidence in Your Abilities

Paper trading is and forever will lack one very important element: emotions. Everyone has emotions that they will need to trade within and learn to recognize. Going back, this is the reason many traders fail when they first start. The new trader has built a great plan that includes trading rules, entry and exit signals and invested time and money to make this work. But as soon as the first trade has been placed in the market with real money, all of the rules can take second place to one's gut. Suddenly, the emotions suggest intervention because the stock is not immediately behaving the way you foresaw; therefore, the plan must be flawed and if you do nothing you will lose everything. You certainly do not want to turn a blind eye to a trade that is moving against your plan, just do not overreact. Allow the ebb and flow of the plan to take place before you execute your exit.

It is much easier to paper trade and be profitable with a lopsided winning percentage, but it is also easy to reset the paper trading account if it all goes bad. This luxury does not exist with real brokerage accounts. You cannot go back and change the outcome by saying *I would have gotten out here* or *I would not have really made that trade because...*

The first real trade placed should be done after paper trading to make sure that the entry and exit points have been established. The first real trade should be made as soon as you realize losing trades will happen and understand when to exit the trade. The first trade should be made as soon as you have a clear trading plan that includes trading rules and strategies to implement. The first real trade should be made sooner than later.

Please do not misunderstand, paper trading is fantastic and has a value to every trader, however, no one is ever able to retire from the profits made while paper trading. If that were the case, many real estate investors would have retired with the blue, green, and pink money they pulled from their *Monopoly* game years ago.

When is it time to move from paper trading to real trading? This is a question that will be uniquely answered with each individual. The fact is you will need to make the call. Often it is when you have explored all the pitfalls and potential successes from trading and feel ready to make the trade, even if it means losing everything on that trade, which is not likely to happen with a properly designed exit strategy.

Checklist to Actual Trading

- ☐ Funded Brokerage Account
- ☐ Trading Rules
- ☐ Strategy Outline
- ☐ Trading Goals
- ☐ Realistic Expectations
- ☐ Trade Journal/Trade History

The list of items that should be considered when moving from paper trading to real trading should contain some basic elements. For instance, the trading rules that were discussed in earlier chapters are partly derived from goals and expectations of trading. Another is the ability to lock in on a strategy and understand the pros and cons of that strategy. Many times this understanding of your chosen strategy comes from a proper trade journal or trade log.

A trade journal should contain every trade made, good, bad and everything in between. The journal becomes the foot print to success in trading that can offer insight only found from experience. Realizing the value of trade tracking will come when the same stock that was traded perhaps months or years ago comes back on your possible trade radar. When this happens, you will be able to compare the behavior of the stock currently to how it behaved in the past trade. Compare the good, and the bad things that happened, how long the trade took to develop, how much of a price move occurred during the trade, did the trade exit early, late or as projected, how well does the stock respond to support and/or resistance points, and the list can go on and on.

Learn from your successful trades as well as your unsuccessful trades to repeat the good and be aware of what can make the next trade go bad. No matter how you come to the point of the next trade it will be you that must take the risk and make the decision to pull the trigger on executing the trade.

Armed with Bullish, Bearish and Neutral Strategies, it is time that you make the call and understand what it means as a trader with clear expectations and a working knowledge of your strategy to buy and sell for profits.

Chapter 8

Conclusion

The one thing I hope was gained from reading and studying the contents of the earlier chapters is that you feel prepared to execute a trade following a well designed plan. You enter into a Covered Call trade understanding the potential profit, the time it will take to complete the trade and collect the profit, and what to do if things do not go as forecasted.

The time of being intimidated by large institutions, confusing terms, misleading rules and regulations are over. Profits will be made in the market tomorrow by someone…why not you?

I recall what led me to making my first trade in the stock market. The process of buying low and selling high was something I learned earlier in life but it took some time to apply it to the stock market. While in High School, I was fascinated with sports and more specifically sports trading cards. I would regularly purchase the Beckett Monthly price guide (a magazine issued monthly with the current prices of nearly all the baseball trading cards available) and check the increased value of the baseball cards I had in my collection. I would add to my collection by purchasing packs of trading cards from the local drug store or sports memorabilia store. As my collection grew I began to trade other students for cards in their collection based on the value in the Beckett Monthly price guide.

The baseball card trading continued until I attended my first sports card and memorabilia convention near Chicago, IL. While at this convention I found that even though the Beckett Monthly price guide gave a value for the baseball card, it meant little if a vendor at the convention was not willing to pay cash for the baseball card. This taught me my first valuable lesson: If there is no demand for your product (baseball card), there is no real value (cash). The demand is similar to the volume of a stock and represents where the stock market demand is and at what degree.

Armed with this new knowledge of which baseball cards could actually be converted into cash, regardless of the price guide, I headed back to my fellow students. I would trade my cards with equal or less value for cards I knew I could convert into cash at the conventions. Based on the actual purchase price of the small packs purchased at the local drug store of unknown cards, I could turn a small investment into a reasonable profit and still continue to build my collection of sports cards. Here was the second lesson learned: Learn and understand the marketplace to buy low and sell high.

Years of repeating this process went by. At this point the stock market was not even a consideration. Finally, while attending Purdue University in pursuit of my Finance degree, I happened to enroll in Dr. Pat Obi's class. During one of our class discussions we were learning about P/E Ratios. Dr. Obi got on the internet and located the real-time data for multiple companies traded in the stock market. That was my first glimpse into what has since become a lifelong interest: The Stock Market.

Later, during a conversation in Dr. Obi's office, I asked the question probably asked many times before…*what is the stock market all about and how does it work?* After he answered my questions I left remembering one important message: If you want to know what trading in the stock market is all about, you need to open an account and make a trade. I did just that. I opened a brokerage account where I could place trades through the internet, which at that time was relatively new and slow, using a dial-up internet connection.

The years that followed were spent gaining valuable experience and, more importantly, establishing the rules within the covered call trading strategy.

The years that follow for you should start just as simply, much as the concept of trading sports cards was for me, then quickly move toward being actively involved in the investing and trading in the stock and option markets just as I was encouraged to do while in college.

Remember these few key steps and guidelines…

Search for a broker with the features you want as well as for potential stocks and options that fit your strategy criteria.

Research each potential trade using both fundamental and technical analysis.

Manage each stock for the strategy it fits and don't force a stock into a strategy it doesn't fit into.

Keep it simple, keep it consistent, and fight to keep the emotions out so you can stay within your strategy toward profits and reliable cash flow.

Happy Trading…Happy Retirement

Made in the USA
Monee, IL
04 November 2026

67383103R00075